Historical and Cultural Dictionaries of Asia Series

edited by Basil C. Hedrick

1. *Saudi Arabia*, by Carroll I. Riley. 1972

2. *Nepal*, by Basil C. and Anne K. Hedrick. 1972

Historical and Cultural Dictionary of
SAUDI ARABIA

by

CARROLL L. RILEY

Historical and Cultural Dictionaries of Asia, No. 1

The Scarecrow Press, Inc.
Metuchen, N.J.   1972

Library of Congress Cataloging in Publication Data

Riley, Carroll L
    Historical and cultural dictionary of Saudi Arabia.

    (Historical and cultural dictionaries of Asia series,
1)
    1. Saudi Arabia--Dictionaries and encyclopedias.
I. Title. II. Series.
DS203.R53   953'.8'003   72-5584
ISBN 0-8108-0534-0

EDITOR'S FOREWORD

The author of the Historical and Cultural Dictionary of Saudi Arabia accepted the writing assignment to select, in a somewhat arbitrary manner--based on his experience and knowledge--the materials for inclusion in this volume. The intent of this volume, as is the case for the entire Historical and Cultural Dictionaries of Asia series, is to provide a source where both the scholar and the casual and interested reader may find factual, somewhat balanced, and certainly helpful information pertinent to the nation in question.

This volume is not intended to be an exhaustive listing, nor should it be viewed as an encyclopedia. It is intended as a "ready reference" work which, when used with other bibliographic tools, should prove to be an invaluable source of information. Clearly, the present volume meets all of the criteria set forth above. This is certainly the most complete and lucid set of facts and statistics concerning Saudi Arabia yet seen by the editor. In selecting his materials for entry, the author has obviously kept the Westerner in mind, entering items which would normally cause the casual researcher painstaking hours of digging in libraries and archives; yet he has not sacrificed the flavor of the history and culture of the nation.

The author of Saudi Arabia, Dr. Carroll L. Riley, is most admirably suited for writing this work, for he has long had an in-depth interest in the Near East and has done research on and written about various circum-Mediterranean lands over a period of years. Dr. Riley is particularly interested in anthropology, ethnohistory, ethnology, and history. Presently, he is Professor and Curator of Anthropology at Southern Illinois University at Carbondale. He has previously been on the faculty at the Universities of Colorado and North Carolina, and has served as a consultant to, or worked for, various federal and state government agencies. Riley has also been a practicing field archaeologist in several nations about the world. To date, he has authored or edited seven major books and has had published some thirty journal articles. He is also editor of several series in divergent fields. A prolific but careful writer, Dr. Riley's writings may be relied upon to be as factual as is humanly possible.

In this book about Saudi Arabia, Dr. Riley has carefully innovated a system of orthography which should, by all standards, represent a departure in the transliteration of Arabic to English. He explains his technique, simple but effective as it is, in his introduction. It is conceivable that other authors and Arabicists may see the value in the system presented here.

Inevitably, there will be some item omitted which some readers will feel to be an error. Further, there may be an occasional question concerning the interpretation given in a given entry. The editor will be pleased to receive suggestions of a substantive and constructive nature for the improvement of this, or any volume in the series.

Basil C. Hedrick
Director
University Museum
Southern Illinois University at Carbondale

iv

INTRODUCTION

The history of Saudi Arabia can only be understood in the wider context of Arabian history and that, in turn, is closely intertwined with the history of a great religion, Islam. In this dictionary I have tried to maintain a balance between the particular events of the kingdom of Faisal ibn Abdul Aziz and his illustrious predecessors, and the wider events, some of which shaped the lives of a large segment of mankind. Though I have listed the major personages of the Saudi family and other individuals, Arabian or foreign, that have played an important part in the history of the region, my concentration has been on events, places and things--this is a cultural dictionary, not a dictionary of biography.

In this book I have cross-indexed whenever it seemed necessary for clarity. Individual entries that concern the organization of affairs or the uses of life in Saudi Arabia e.g., EDUCATION, COMMUNICATIONS, refer to that country unless otherwise spelled out. On the other hand, certain wide headings (e.g., HISTORY) are included under the larger rubric, ARABIA. Dates, unless otherwise noted, are A.D.; Hegira dates are always stated as such.

In the spelling of Arabic words I have chosen the simple (perhaps even brutal) expedient of ignoring all dia-criticals. This extreme simplification occasionally leads to grammatical distortion as when an elided article is moved back to the preceding word. My interest however is always in ready identification, not in phonetic precision. The Arabic article al is generally omitted; exceptions to this include names where it has become imbedded via translation into regular English usage. Generally I have tried to use spellings that are found in the press or in those popular books on Arabia aimed at an educated lay public rather than Arabicists. The Saudi Arabian Ministry of Information uses the same practices in its English publications. In addition, a number of arbitrary choices had to be made. For example, I chose Koran over Quran or al-Quran, Muhammad over Mohammad, Moslem over Muslim, etc. There is no particular pattern in these choices.

A number of persons have been helpful in preparation of this book. I especially wish to thank Henry J. Petraki and Mazin Abbass for their guidance in Arabic language matters and John Clifford and Charles Holliday for aid in library research. I. Mosley, Third Secretary of the Saudi Arabian Embassy, Washington, D. C. gave much kind help and advice. William Sands of the Middle East Institute, Father A. Jamme of Catholic University and Archie Van Peursem of the Aramco offices, Washington, D. C. also made helpful suggestions.

The mechanical task of preparing the manuscript was done by Jon S. Williams, Maureen O. Szoke, Mary Ann Guyer and Susan Fry. Virginia Karnes and Theresa A. Page also helped with various aspects of manuscript preparation.

Lastly, special thanks go to my assistant, Donna Kathleen Abbass, who worked at all stages in the evolution of this dictionary and whose contributions were both mechanical and substantive.

C. L. R.

ABA. A loose sleeveless camel's hair cloak worn by both men and women in Saudi Arabia.

ABAL. Small bush that grows in the dune areas of the Rub al Khali: Calligonum sp.

ABDUL AZIZ IBN ABDUL RAHMAN AL FAISAL AL SAUD see IBN SAUD

ABDUL AZIZ IBN MITAB IBN RASHID. Nephew of Muhammad ibn Abdulla ibn Rashid, Abdul Aziz became ruler of Hail in 1897, but was killed in a skirmish with the Saudi forces in 1906.

ABDUL AZIZ I IBN SAUD (1766-1803). The Imam of Dariya who laid the foundations for the first Saudi Empire. A strong adherent of Muhammad ibn Abdul Wahhab, Abdul Aziz extended Saudi control over much of eastern Arabia. A dramatic event late in his life was the sack and destruction of Karbala in Iraq, a city which contained the tomb of the Shia saint, Hussein ibn Ali. (See ISLAM.) In early October, 1803, the eighty-two year old Imam was assassinated in the mosque at Dariya by a survivor of the Karbala massacre.

ABDULLA (Abd Allah, "Slave of God"). Member of the Quraish tribe of Mecca, son of Abdul Mutallib, and father of Muhammad the Prophet. Abdulla died before the birth of his famous son.

ABDULLA IBN AL ABBAS MOSQUE. Historical mosque at the Hejazi city of Taif.

ABDULLA IBN FAISAL. Son of Faisal ibn Turki ibn Saud who--during a very confused period of Saudi history--contended with his brother, Saud, for rule of Nejd. Abdulla is generally supposed to have headed the Saud family from 1865 to 1871 and from 1875 to 1889.

1

Abdulla's brother, Saud, was in control from 1871 to 1875, at which year he was killed in a desert raid. Abdulla spent much of the time after 1875 as a virtual prisoner of Muhammad ibn Rashid of Hail. In 1889 Abdulla, now very ill, was allowed to return from Hail to Riyadh, where he soon died. A younger brother, Abdul Rahman, who had ruled for a few months in 1875 now, accepted the headship of the Saudi family. However a Rashid commander, the notorious Salim al Subhan, continued to rule at Riyadh.

ABDULLA IBN FAISAL IBN ABDUL AZIZ. Eldest son of King Faisal of Saudi Arabia by his first wife, Sultana bint Ahmad al Sudaini.

ABDULLA IBN IBRAHIM AL NAJDI. Moslem scholar of the early eighteenth century who lived in the Hasa. Muhammad ibn Abdul Wahhab, founder of Wahhabism, studied with him for a time, probably in the 1730's. Abdulla was later to be known as al Madani because he made the city of Medina the center of his teaching.

ABDULLA IBN JILUWI see IBN JILUWI

ABDULLA IBN RASHID. Last independent ruler at Hail. Abdulla ascended the throne in 1920 but the city and area fell the following year to Ibn Saud.

ABDULLA IBN SAUD. Saudi ruler who came to power in 1814 at the death of his father, Saud II Ibn Saud. The entire four year period of Abdulla's rule was spent in a struggle against the Egyptians under Muhammad Ali Pasha. In September, 1818, after a courageous resistance of six months, Abdulla surrendered Dariya, the Saudi capital, to Ibrahim Pasha, the son of Muhammad. Abdulla, himself, was taken captive and eventually sent to Istanbul, where he was executed by order of the Sultan.

ABDULLA SULAIMAN see ARAMCO

ABDUL MUTALLIB (Abd al Muttalib). Grandfather (father's father) of Muhammad, and son of Hashim. The Prophet Muhammad lived with Abdul Mutallib as a boy.

ABDUL RAHMAN IBN FAISAL. Head of the House of Saud after the death of an older brother, Abdulla, in 1889.

Abdul Rahman ruled Riyadh under the Rashids from 1889 to 1891 but in that year he was forced to flee to the coastal area, where he eventually took up residence in Kuwait. Abdul Rahman was never again to play a leading part in Saudi affairs but he lived to see a famous son, Abdul Aziz ibn Abdul Rahman ibn Saud, restore the fortunes of the Saudi family and to build the Kingdom of Saudi Arabia.

ABDUL WAHHAB IBN MUHAMMAD IBN SULAIMAN IBN ALI AL TAMINI. Abdul Wahhab ibn Sulaiman, who flourished around 1700, was the father of the religious reformer Muhammad ibn Abdul Wahhab. Abdul Wahhab ibn Sulaiman was a member of the Masharifa clan which claimed relationship to the Prophet Muhammad in a cognate line. The father of the reformer lived in the principality of Ayaina which at that time (early eighteenth century) had an alliance with, and perhaps was under the loose rule of the Bani Khalid, a tribe that ruled in the Hasa. Abdul's family belonged to the Tamim tribe which had lived for centuries in northeastern Arabia.

ABHA.   The capital of the highland district of Asir.   The city lies some 8,000 feet above sea level, and has an estimated population of 30,000.

ABQAIQ.   An oil settlement some forty miles southwest of Dhahran, and one of the centers of ARAMCO oil operations.

ABRAQ.   A sand hill.   The Burgan oil field of Kuwait takes its name from burgan, the plural of abraq.

ABU ARISH.   A small city in the extreme south of coastal Asir.   Abu Arish is some twenty miles east of the port city of Jizan and connected to it by an all-weather highway.

ABU DHABI.   One of the Trucial States (as of December, 1971, a member of the Union of Arab Emirates). Also name of the main town in the area.

ABU JENABIYA (Sideways going father).   The popular Arab name for the desert horned viper (Cerastes cornutus) found in northern Arabia and the Sinai Desert.

ABU TALIB. Brother of Muhammad's father, Abdulla, guardian of the Prophet during his early years, and his protector in the period of the early revelations. Abu Talib died, probably in A.D. 619. See also ARABIA, HISTORY OF--ISLAMIC PERIOD.

ADEN. A former British colony in southern Arabia consisting of the port city of Aden (population approximately 200,000) east of the Bab el Mandeb Straits. The city and the adjacent Western and Eastern Aden Protectorates were merged into a Federation of South Arabia in 1962. In 1967-1968 an independent Peoples Republic of Southern Yemen replaced the Federation.

AELIUS GALLUS see GALLUS, AELIUS

AFJA. In Arabic, desert terrain where bushes or other desert plants have taken root, thus holding the sand.

AFLAJ. An agricultural district in Nejd, sixty to seventy miles south and east of Riyadh.

AGAL. The rope-like band worn by men to hold in place the headpiece called kaffiyeh or ghutra.

AGRICULTURE AND LAND USE. Under the direction of the Ministry of Agriculture and Water, the Saudi Government is developing a number of agricultural projects, especially in the Kharj and Aflaj areas south of Riyadh, in the Hasa, in Najran, and in various parts of Hejaz and Asir. The latter province was once an agriculturally rich area and large land reclamation plans in the Wadi Jizan and around Abha will greatly increase the agricultural wealth of this part of Arabia.

At present the Ministry of Agriculture and Water has an annual budget of eighty-five million dollars for the various projects, particularly those in land reclamation.

AIDH. Ruling family in Abha who, in 1919, called Ibn Saud to help in their fight against Muhammad al Idrisi. Saudi forces occupied Asir in 1920 but remained in control of the highland portions of Asir. In 1924 the Aidh leaders rebelled against Ibn Saud but were quickly defeated by a Saudi army led by Prince Faisal. Asir was finally brought completely under Saudi control in 1930.

AIN. An Arabic word for well or spring.

AIN HIT. A water hole south of Riyadh where the Ibn Saud forces camped on the 1902 raid that rescued Riyadh from Rashidi forces. In 1937 American oil engineers working for Aramco discovered Bahrein cap rock (the strata that overlies oil bearing formations) at the bottom of Ain Hit.

AJAMA. One of the Trucial States, since December, 1971, a member of the Union of Arab Emirates.

AJLAN. Governor of Riyadh under the Rashids. Ajlan was killed in Ibn Saud's raid in 1902 by Abdulla ibn Jiluwi, a cousin of the future king.

AJMAN. Large tribe in eastern Nejd who were implicated in several rebellions against King Ibn Saud in the time around World War I.

AKH. Arabic word meaning "brother." The plural Akhwan, or, more commonly, Ikhwan, collectively denotes the groups of Wahhabi Bedouin settled by Ibn Saud in agricultural towns.

AKHDAR MOUNTAINS (Green Mountains). Mountain range in northern Oman and Muscat on the Gulf of Oman, with peaks rising to 10,000 feet.

AKHWAN see IKHWAN

ALAMAIN. The markers a few miles from Mecca that mark the beginning of sacred territory, beyond which a non-Moslem may not pass.

AL AMIN (The Trustworthy). A surname given Muhammad because of the Prophet's love and devotion for his first wife, the widow Khadija of Mecca.

AL BAQARA (The Cow). Second and longest sura of the Koran. Sura 2 was probably revealed at Medina in the first and second years after the Hegira, though perhaps some verses are from a later period. The Cow Sura is sometimes described as the "little" Koran for it contains the essential points of Muhammad's revelation.

AL FATIHA (The Opening). Also called Fatihatul Kitab (The
Opening of the Scripture) or Ummul Koran (The Es-
sence of the Koran). The sura is also sometimes referred to as Sabaan min al Mathani (Seven of the Oft-
repeated verses). Called the Lord's Prayer of Islam,
Sura 1 is recited at any solemn or important business,
social, or political transaction or other important occasion. It is a very early sura, certainly introduced
by at least the third year of Muhammad's ministry.
The Opening:
> In the name of Allah, the Beneficent, the Merciful
> 1. Praise be to Allah, Lord of the Worlds
> 2. The Beneficent, the Merciful,
> 3. Owner of the Day of Judgment,
> 4. Thee (alone) we worship; Thee (alone) we ask
>   help.
> 5. Show us the straight path,
> 6. The path of those whom Thou has favoured,
> 7. Not (the path) of those who earn Thine anger
>   nor of those who go astray.

ALI IBN SAID MUHAMMAD. Last independent ruler of Asir
from the death of his father, Said, in 1922 till 1925
when he fled the country.

ALIM. A religious scholar or jurist. Plural is Ulema, the
title for the collective religious leaders of Islam or of
a given area within Islam.

AL LAT. This goddess (whose name means "the goddess")
was a major deity of Taif and the surrounding countryside. Meccans also came to sacrifice in the enclo-
sures sacred to her. At her shrines it was forbidden
to shed blood, whether human or animal and even
plants were inviolable. Al Lat seems to be the same
as the Nabataean goddess Alilat mentioned by Herodo-
tus. Al Lat was one of the three goddesses that became the subject of the abrogated verses of the Koran.

AL MAIDA (The Table Spread). Sura 5 of the Koran. The
third verse of this sura is considered to be the last
utterance of the Prophet Muhammad as revealed in the
Koran. The verse names the religion Al Islam, "The
Surrender to Allah."

ALPHABET (ARABIC)   see ARABIC SCRIPT

AL RAMLAH. An alternate name of the Rub al Khali; sometimes the plural, Al Rimal, is used.

AL UZZA. A major goddess worshipped in the Hejaz in the period before and at the time of Muhammad. Al Uzza was the planet Venus as the morning star. The name refers to her might and glory and she was the most venerated deity among the Quraish at Mecca, Muhammad himself offering sacrifices to her during his youth. Al Uzza's main shrine was at Nakhla east of Mecca. According to tradition, human sacrifice was occasionally offered to Al Uzza. Al Uzza was one of the three "daughters of Allah" that were the subjects of the abrogated verses of the Koran.

AL WAQIDI. Died A.D. 822. Compiler of the Maghazi or history of the campaigns of the Prophet Muhammad.

AMINA. The mother of Muhammad. Amina saw very little of her son for, acting according to tribal tradition and perhaps also because of poverty and sickness (her husband having died before Muhammad's birth), she turned him over to a Bedouin shepherd's wife to raise. At the age of six (probably in 577) Muhammad was returned to his mother but she died very shortly afterwards.

AMMAR MINE see GOLD PRODUCTION

ANAIZA see UNAIZA

ANAZA TRIBE. One of the largest tribes of Saudi Arabia with branches in Nejd and also in Iraq and Syria. The Saudi family is from the Masaleekh branch of this large tribal group.

ANNO HIJRAE (A.H.). The calendrical notation in Islam equivalent to the Christian A.D. The Hegira, or removal of the Islamic colony from Mecca to Medina, took place in A.D. 622, which, thus, became the year 1 A.H. in the Muslim calendar.

ANTARA IBN SHADDAD AL ABSI. A legendary hero of the Ayyam al Arab period, the last century or so before Islam. Antara ibn Shaddad al Absi was a poet and warrior who was born a slave, his mother having been a Black concubine of a tribal chief. Freed by his

father, Antara became a brilliant exemplar of Bedouin
values.   Interestingly, Antara seems to have been a
Christian, though the traditional character of the
sources makes this kind of information rather uncertain.

AQIQ GHAMID MINE   see GOLD PRODUCTION

AQIQ, WADI OF   see MEDINA

ARABIA, FAUNA OF.   Native animals of the Arabian peninsula tend to have African affinities.   Included are a
series of desert grazing animals, the most common
being the gazelle.   One species of antelope, the Oryx
beatrix is common, especially in the Rub al Khali, and
a single species of ibex is also found.   Rodents include
several varieties of hares and rabbits.   In the east and
south of Arabia are several varieties of old world mon-
keys (Cercopithecidae) especially baboons.   Other small
animals include the skunk, badger, porcupine and
hedgehog.   The jerboa, or kangaroo rat, is common
through all the desert areas of Arabia.
   Carnivores include the wolf, jackel, fox, hyena and
mongoose, and among the felines, wildcats, leopards
and a few cheetas.   The lion has long since disappeared from Arabia as from other parts of the Near
East.
   A series of carnivorous birds are common to Arabia including eagles, hawks, and falcons--the latter
tamed and trained for falconry.   The owl, raven and
vulture are found and a variety of game birds including
sand grouse, doves, pigeons, partridges, quail and
lesser bustard.   Until very recently ostrich lived in
the desert areas of Arabia, and one shot in 1938 near
the Saudi Arabia-Iraq boundary weighed 300 pounds.
Presumably the ostrich is extinct today but was quite
common as late as the 1930's.   Over-hunting for plu-
mage and for sport has led to the disappearance of
this bird.   Smaller birds include the hoopoe, nightin-
gale, lark, sparrow, and swallow.   Numbers of ducks
of various kinds migrate in winter to areas where
there is sufficient water.
   The Arabian desert supports a number of reptiles
including the desert monitor, and various geckos and
skinks.   The horned viper of the genus Cerastes and
also vipers of the genus Echis are extremely specialized for desert life with scales forming serrated
ridges that allow the creature to bury itself by a series

of lateral shovelling motions that throw dirt over its back.   A species of true cobra is also found in Arabia; this is the narrow hooded Egyptian asp (Naja haje) famed as the snake with which Cleopatra ended her life. Like all cobras the asp is exceedingly venomous. There are also poisonous water snakes in Arabia and various harmless varieties.

Freshwater fish are not important in arid Arabia though a number of species are found.   In the Persian Gulf are king mackerel, grouper, barracuda, and saw-fish.   Sharks are also very common, as are sardines. Various sea mammals are also found in these waters including dolphins, and an occasional whale.   An im-portant food animal in Persian Gulf waters is the shrimp which is eaten by both town people and desert Bedouins.   Because of its greater salinity the Red Sea has less sea life than has the Persian Gulf, but fishing is important at various points.

Insects and arachnids are very common in the des-ert with a number of scorpions, spiders, ants, milli-pedes, and centipedes.   A serious problem, recorded from early historic times and continuing to the present, is the cyclic swarm of locusts.   These insects can destroy vegetation over large areas; however they are also roasted and eaten, especially by Bedouins.

Domestic animals are extremely important in Ara-bia because of the great emphasis on nomadic herding life, especially in the desert areas.   The single-humped camel is perhaps the most important animal, especially among the true Bedouin.   A breed called the Umaniya produced by the Al Murra tribe, whose territory stretches over much of the Rub al Khali, is considered the most valuable because of its endurance. The camel's main value in the desert comes from the fact that it can live and function for several days with-out water.   Camel hair is also used for weaving and young camels are eaten.

Like camels, horses are traditionally associated with Arabia.   Basically war animals, their value has been somewhat lessened in recent years because of a decline in raiding and because of the use of powerful, modern rifles which makes their speed and mobility of less account.   The Arabian horse, however, remains a status symbol in modern Saudi Arabia.   The donkey is used by many of the less wealthy nomadic tribes as a beast of burden.   Sheep and goats are everywhere important, producing milk, meat, and wool.   The cow,

however, is not an important animal. Most of the cat-
tle are Brahman type and tend to be rather small in
size.
    The Arabian saluki (from the Arabic, Saluqi) a long
limbed, long bodied graceful hound with feathered ears,
legs, and tail, is extensively used in hunting. This
breed of dog is perhaps better known in Egypt where
it has been bred from early times.
    Other domestic animals in Arabia include fowls, es-
pecially the chicken (Gallus sp.) which is utilized for
both food and eggs.

ARABIA FELIX. That portion of the Arabian Peninsula that
    consists of present day Asir, Yemen and the western
    Hadhramaut. The name was given southwestern Arabia
    by the Greco-Roman peoples because of the fine climate
    and riches in agricultural goods and in spices.

ARABIA, FLORA OF. This varies considerably with altitude
    and to some degree with latitude. Generally speaking
    the plant life of Arabia is related to Africa rather
    than to South Asia. In the higher elevations in west-
    ern and southern Arabia are juniper forests. In south-
    ern Arabia also appear coconut and daum palms. Trees of
    the genera Acacia and Mimosa, the carob (Ceratonia sp.),
    and the evergreen shrub tamarisk (Tamarix sp.) are also
    found. Several species of the succulent, Euphorbia occur
    in southern Arabia especially in the Yemen as does the red
    flowered Adenium obesum. Zizyphus jujuba (the "Jub-
    jub") often growing to tree size is found in all parts
    of Arabia. Various members of the genus Aloe are
    also found on the peninsula.
        In the sand deserts are bushes and shrubs of vari-
    ous kinds, some important as anchors to the restless
    dunes, especially in the Rub al Khali and in the Nafud
    to the North. Various grasses and flowering plants
    include some of the mustards that spring up after
    every rain. In some parts of Arabia truffles are
    found.
        Cultivated plants include wheats, barley, and millet,
    and melons of various kinds. A number of garden
    plants, including radishes, species of pumpkins and
    squashes, gourds, onions, leaks, and cucumbers, grow
    in the Hejaz, in the highlands of Asir and Yemen and
    in the oases in the desert. The date palm is impor-
    tant all over the peninsula and a basic food in the
    area. Many of the tree fruits--peaches, apricots,

pomegranates, and figs occur in the oases and in mountain valleys while the apple and quince are found in the highlands. Various spice plants are grown in south Arabia and coffee, introduced from east Africa in the fourteenth century, grows on the mountain slopes of Asir and Yemen. The stimulant gat (Catha edulis), a shrub that somewhat resembles the European privet in appearance, is grown especially in Yemen where the habit of chewing the leaves is widespread. Tobacco is sporadically grown in southern Arabia, especially in the Hadhramaut, although Wahhabi puritanism discourages smoking in Saudi Arabia.

ARABIA, GEOGRAPHY OF. Arabia, the largest peninsula of Asia, has an area of 1,027,000 square miles of which Saudi Arabia has some 872,000 square miles, Yemen some 75,000 square miles and the remaining 80,000 square miles includes Kuwait, Qatar, Muscat and Oman, the Trucial states and South Yemen. Within Saudi Arabia are four main provinces; Nejd with 650,000 square miles (including the bleak Rub al Khali), Hejaz 135,000 square miles, Hasa (Eastern Province) 41,000 square miles and Asir with 40,000 square miles. There is, in addition, the arid Northern Frontier Province, not completely charted. The total population is about twelve million, of which approximately seven million live in Saudi Arabia, four million in Yemen and the remaining million in the other small states.
    The Arabian peninsula is, generally speaking, an eastward tilting plateau, the western edge having a series of highlands extending from northwest to southeast that rise sharply some ten to fifteen miles from the Red Sea coast, and averaging thirty miles in width. These highlands constitute the heartland of the Hejaz, Asir and Yemen-Aden. These highlands trend upward in elevation from north to south. In the north, elevations average about 5000 feet, while in the Jibil of Yemen the average height of the mountains is about 9000 feet and the highest peak in the peninsula is 12,336 feet. Along the south coast of Arabia is an east west tending range in the old provinces of Aden and the Hadhramaut.
    Only the mountain country of the southwest part of the peninsula can be considered well watered, with the area around Sana near Nebi Shuaib receiving over twenty inches of rainfall per year. The rest of the peninsula is desert or semi-desert.

There are four major groups of permanent water holes: Al Hasa south of Kuwait, Najran near the Saudi Arabian-Yemen border, Kharj, south southeast and Al Aflaj southwest of Riyadh. The portion of Arabia east of the western mountain wall consists of the Nejd, a region of hard desert surrounded by great areas of sand desert; the northern Nafud, which is connected to the barren Rub al Khali in the south by a river of sand, the four hundred mile long Dahna. East of this region are the coastal areas of Kuwait, Hasa, Qatar, the Trucial States and Oman, a very dry area excepting for the uplands of Oman where peaks rise to over 9,000 feet and where annual precipitation in a few areas may reach twelve to fifteen inches a year. North of the Nafud is the stony waste of the Syrian desert which extends well beyond Arabia proper.

The peninsula has no permanent rivers but contains several long systems of wadis or intermittent streams, especially in the Nejd. This area is drained by three great systems, the Wadi Rumma-Batin system in the north, the Surra-Hanifa system in the center and the Dawasir system in the south. The first two empty into the Persian Gulf and the third disappears in the sandy wastes of the Rub al Khali.

Climatically, the highlands of Asir and Yemen and the western Hadhramaut have rich potentialities for agriculture because of fertile soil and rainfall in the mountains adequate to support irrigation. This is the Arabia Felix of ancient times. Somewhat similar conditions exist in that portion of Oman-Muscat that faces the Gulf of Oman (The Batina coast), for rains falling on the Akhdar mountains produce enough rainfall for irrigation.

Because of its latitude, low incidence of rainfall, and general low elevation, Arabia is one of the hottest areas of the world. In the Nejd temperatures in summer may rise to 120° F. or above, though nights are cool because of the low humidity. Winters in the Nejd are pleasant with frosts at night in the higher elevations. The mountainous areas of western and southern Arabia have dry, pleasant climates except that Yemen and the Aden area are touched by the monsoons and have considerable rainfall in the summer months (June-September) especially at higher altitudes. The coastal areas, however, both east and west, have high humidity and great heat and produce the disagreeable climate often associated with Arabia.

ARABIA, GEOLOGY OF. Because of the tremendous impor-
tance of oil in the modern world and because of the
oil riches of the peninsula, Arabia is reasonably well
known geologically. The major features in eastern
Arabia are a series of sedimentary limestone and sand-
stones, largely Mesozoic in origin, that gradually deep-
en as they extend eastward, reaching a depth of 20,000
feet or more at the Persian Gulf. It is in these deposits that the oil riches of the peninsula are mainly
found. Westward is an ancient shield that extends into
Africa; it is made up of metamorphosed rocks cut with
more recent igneous deposits. The western mountains
of Arabia are largely composed of granitic and other
igneous materials. Volcanic activity still continues to
some degree in western Arabia. The area of the Gulf
of Aqaba and the Red Sea is a rift valley system that
extends northward through the Jordan valley and southward through the lakes area of eastern Africa.

ARABIA, HISTORY OF--EARLY PERIOD. Man settled quite
early in Arabia, for there is evidence of pre-Sapiens
human activity in the peninsula. In Post Pleistocene
times, however, Arabia has generally been peripheral,
first, to the advanced cultures of the Fertile Crescent
and Egypt, then to the wider world of the Middle East.
Still and all, Arabia's influence has been felt directly
or indirectly throughout much of recent history.
    By 3000 B.C. the region from the highlands of Iraq
westward and southward to the Mediterranean Coast
and into upper Egypt was becoming urbanized, with advanced technologies, use of metallurgy, sophisticated
architecture, complex social and political organization,
priestly religious cults and the beginnings of writing.
Much of this area, even at this early date, was settled by peoples speaking Semitic languages, though
Egyptian was a member of the related Hamitic linguistic group, and at least one non-Semitic language, that
of Sumeria, was spoken throughout the lower Tigris-
Euphrates valley. In the next 1500 years Sumerian
was to disappear as a living language and Semitic
tongues spread into this area as well.
    It has been suggested that the homeland of Semitic
speech was in fact the Arabian peninsula. This theory
does not conflict with the known distributions of Semitic languages in historic times, but, in the absence of

written records and in the fragmentary state of Arabian
archaeology, no final conclusions can now be drawn.
A number of Semitic languages past and present are
known and can be conveniently divided into three major
geographical groups. Northeast Semitic included Akka-
dian, recorded in Mesopotamia in the third millenium
B. C., and daughter languages like Old Babylonian and
Old Assyrian. A second group, the Northwest Semitic,
included or includes Canaanite, Hebrew, Phoenician,
Aramaic, Syraic and such lesser known languages as
Moabite, Nabataean Palmyrene, and Mandaean. Some
of these languages are identified from inscriptions of
the second millenium B. C. and were written in early
alphabetic scripts. The third Semitic group of languages is called Southwest Semitic, the two major languages being Arabic and Ethiopic. Within the family
of Southwest Semitic, Arabic can be divided into two
major dialects, northern and southern. Such southern
Arabian kingdoms as the Sabaeans and Minaeans had a
literate class who, utilizing a South Semitic alphabet,
left inscriptions dating from the eighth century B. C.,
while the Safaitic, Lihyanite, Dedanite, and Thamudene
scripts in northern Arabia, also variants of a South
Semitic alphabet, may reflect an early form of northern Arabic.

Kingdoms of considerable wealth, apparently located
somewhere in northern Arabia, are suggested in the
Assyrian records of the Assyrian King Shalmaneser III
(around 854 B. C.) and of Tiglathpileser III (734 B. C.).
In each case the specific ruler mentioned, "Gindibu the
Arabian" and "Samsi Queen of Arabia, " controlled
large armies and owned thousands of animals.

The earliest documented high cultures from southern
Arabia are those of the Yemenite Minaean and Sabaean
kingdoms centered at Main and Saba respectively, and
the less well-known kingdoms of Qataban and Hadhramaut to the east. All of these seem to have been influenced by peoples from northern Arabia who pene-
trated to the south, perhaps in the last half of the
second millenium B. C. The rise of Yemen was surely
connected to the development of camel domestication
which dates from about 1000 B. C. The powerful ad-
vantages in a desert land given by the camel can
scarcely be overestimated, for the beast can carry
heavy burdens (four to five hundred pounds), can be
ridden over long distances at high speeds, and, if necessary, can go for days without water. The stories of

the Queen of Sheba who, according to tradition was from the Yemen, mention camels and the Shalmaneser inscription about "Gindibu the Arab" tells us that he led camel men against the Assyrians in the Syrian Desert.

Rooted in camel caravans, the kingdoms centered at Main (the Minaean) and at Saba (the Sabaean) began to act as middlemen for the spices produced in the Hadhramaut and perhaps in India. At some point Saba absorbed Main and extended her control by the use of naval power over the east African Horn. From a new capital, Marib, east of modern Sana, the Sabaeans controlled much of southern Arabia.

The Oman area of southwestern Arabia meanwhile had been at least partially brought under the control of the Persian Empire perhaps from the time of Cyrus the Great. Northern coastal Arabia has a much longer history; from at least the third millenium B.C. the island of Bahrein was a transshipment point for goods originating in Mesopotamia to the north. It was the Dilmun of the Sumerians and recent archaeological work has made it clear that the island had active and advanced cultures, and was tremendously important in the Mesopotamian scheme of things. Less is known of the adjacent coasts (Kuwait, Hasa, and Qatar) but they too were somewhat influenced by Mesopotamia. A vaguely defined area known as the "Sealand" is mentioned in early Mesopotamian documents and this may have included part of northeastern Arabia. Northern Arabia seems, from at least the third millenium, to have been a reservoir of nomadic tribesmen that periodically flooded the fertile lands both to the east and the west. The Amorites who overran southern Mesopotamia about 2000 B.C., and threatened Palestine and Egypt about this time were most likely from the deserts of northern Arabia.

Archaeology of central Arabia (the Nejd) is in its infancy but, at least by the time of Muhammad, the region was well populated with both nomadic and sedentary tribes. The Hejaz was also well populated, and, clearly, Sabaean influences reached into both Asir and Hejaz. This region was known to the Persians and, after Alexander, was on the periphery of two Greek kingdoms. The Romans were interested in Hejaz; they controlled the Wadi Sirhan Desert and around A.D. 100 established direct rule in Petra, center of the Nabataean state north of the Gulf of Aqaba. Earlier, in 24 B.C., one of Augustus' army commanders, Aelius Gallus, invaded Arabia marching through the Hejaz and Asir to around the present Saudi-Yemen border. He was defeated by one Ilasaros of Saba and the remnants of his army forced northward to the Hejaz.

In the late Roman period the largely Arabian city of Palmyra north of the peninsula in the Syrian Desert oasis of Tadmor, became a considerable power, replacing Petra as the great trade center between Arabia, and the Mediterranean and Mesopotamian world. Originally a Roman client state, Palmyra, after the defeat the Emperor Valerian in A. D. 260 by the Sassanids, made a bid for independence. Under King Odenathus and later under Zenobia, the widow of Odenathus, Palmyra established control over northern Arabia as well as parts of Syria and other nearby areas. The capture of Zenobia by the Roman Emperor Aurelian in 272 ended the hegemony of Palmyra. The power vacuum created by the fall of Palmyra was filled for a time by the Ghassanid kingdom centered in middle Palestine west of the Jordan River. The Ghassanids claimed to have originally come from Yemen, at a time near the end of the third century A. D. The Ghassanids shared power in the Syrian desert area with the Kingdom of the Lakhmids whose capital was at Al Hira on the Lower Euphrates. In the sixth century these two kingdoms acted as buffer states between Byzantium and Sassanid Persia. They were both in a state of decay, however, at the time of the Hegira and were quickly overrun by the Islamic armies a few years later.

Meanwhile, in southern Arabia, the Sabaean power was broken by a resurgent Main to the north and Qataban to the east. The period of the last centuries B. C. is one of great confusion with Hadhramaut, expanding eastward and a new power called Himyar, situated west of present day Aden, also expanding. A composite group--part Himyar and part Saba--sometime around the beginning of the Christian era formed a kingdom of Saba and Dhu Raydan with a capital at Zafar in the area of Yarim north of present day Taiz. The Sabaean element in this kingdom eventually reasserted itself and the capital was shifted to Marib further north. This group also overran much of Hadhramaut.

Meanwhile the Abyssinian state of Axum, which had earlier shared a frontier with Rome on the middle Nile, began to expand across the Red Sea and shortly after A. D. 300 conquered parts of Yemen and Hadhramaut.

This kingdom, called Habashat by the southern Arabians, perhaps introduced Christianity into the area; at any rate a king of Himyar was baptized around A.D. 360. Religious ideas were certainly seeping into southern Arabia, for in the fifth century A.D. there were conversions to Judaism, this religion probably spreading as a direct or indirect result of the diaspora that followed the Hadrian war.

Christian influence in southern Arabia was sufficiently marked for the appointment of Bishop Gregentius around 550, from Monophysite Alexandria to an episcopal see at Zafar, and a large church was constructed at Sana. A complex religious and political struggle involving Jews, Christians, Persians, Axumites and native Himyarites of two or three faiths, developed in the latter part of the sixth century and extended to the Hejaz. In A.D. 570 Abraha, an Axum appointee in Yemen, attacked Mecca itself but was driven away. It was shortly after this that Himyar, where the anti-Christian party now had the upper hand, called on Persia to help drive out the Abyssinians. Persian armies advanced into southern Arabia and established at least nominal Persian control that lasted till the defeat of the Persian Empire at the hands of Islam a half century later.

In the area that now comprises the major part of Saudi Arabia, the Nejd and the Hejaz, there is relatively little known until the rise of Muhammad. Both regions were largely populated by nomadic Bedouin tribes and literacy was minimal. Inscriptions or other direct written documents from the pre-Islamic period in this area are virtually unknown, though this is in part due to the fact that very scanty archaeological work has been done in the area. We must depend largely on traditional and secondary sources for information about the period. No doubt the future will see a greatly expanded knowledge of the key region in pre-Islamic times for oasis settlements in places like Mecca and Medina are certainly old, as are settlements in the Hasa region to the east and, probably in the Wadi Hanifa area, later center of Saudi power and influence.

From sources that are available it would seem that population centers like Mecca, Yathrib (Medina), Taif, Ukaz, Uhud, Khaibar, Tayma, Tubuk and others were growing as trade centers or as cult centers or (especially in the case of Mecca) as both. Probably only ten to twenty percent of the population of the Hejaz was "urbanized" and in the Nejd even less. During the course of the sixth century Mecca gradually established its primacy, becoming more and more the main entrepôt for the distribution of the wealth of Yemen and the goods of the Mediterranean. Mecca had long been a cult center. The goddess Al Uzza (the morning star) had her center in a cave at Nakhla between Mecca and Taif and her cult included human sacrifice. In Mecca itself the well of Zamzam was another such center. According to later legend it once supplied water to Ishmael and Hagar (Ishmael, considered the ancestor of the northern Arabs, was the son of Abraham by his second wife Hagar). The sacred well is located in the center of Mecca near the cube-like building, or Kaaba, which houses the sacred black meteorite. In pre-Islamic times this stone was in some way associated with the god Hubal, represented as an idol in human form.

Other towns of the Hejaz are less well-known than Mecca. Taif, situated some seventy miles east of the sacred city and considerably higher (at 5,500 feet), supplied Mecca with food from its rich oasis fields and groves. Yathrib (Medina) became famous in the early seventh century as the place of refuge of the Prophet and for a little while the center of the expanding Islamic empire. In the sixth century Yathrib seems to have been a major center of Jewish life in northern Arabia. Of the Nejd towns and those in Asir we know very little.

Tribal distribution in Arabia during the century before Islam is somewhat better known. This period, the Jahiliya or "time of ignorance," is described in many later legends and stories and tribal positions of early Islamic days in many cases reflected a situation that had held for a number of generations. It is clear from the records that flickering warfare between tribes was the order of the day and some of these wars lasted for decades.

The major tribe at Mecca was that of the Quraish, at Medina the tribes of Aws and Khazra; in northern Arabia the Kalb, in the northeast part of the peninsula the Bakr and the Taghlib, in central Arabia the Abs, the Dhubyan, and the Dabba and near the Rub al Khali, the Hanifa. In addition, at Yathrib were the important Jewish tribes, the Kainuka, the Nadir, and the Kuraiza.

ARABIA, HISTORY OF--ISLAMIC PERIOD. The Prophet
Muhammad, who was to change the face of Arabia and
much of the world, was born probably in the year A.D.
570 or 571. He was a member of the Quraish tribe
but belonged to the Hashimite clan, less influential than
that of the Abd Sham which later produced the Umayyad
lines of Caliphs. Abdulla, the father of Muhammad,
died before his son's birth. Amina, Muhammad's
mother, died when the future prophet was six. The
duty of raising Muhammad thus fell to Abu Talib, a
brother of Abdulla.

In early life, Muhammad travelled with camel caravans and seems to have visited the trading towns in
northern Arabia, perhaps going as far as the Gulf of
Aqaba or even the Mediterranean. One of his employ-
ers was a merchant's widow, Khadija. Around A.D.
595 when Muhammad was twenty-five years old and
Khadija about forty, the two married. By this marriage Muhammad gained financial security and with it
the leisure to ponder the ideas that were to lead to
Islam. As the years went by Muhammad increasingly
withdrew to caves and other deserted places for medi-
tation, and it was on such an occasion, perhaps in A.
D. 610 that Muhammad received the first revelation.

The new religion developed slowly at first as Muhammad developed a corpus of revealed sayings--the
beginnings of a sacred book. Khadija was the first
convert and the Prophet's cousin, Ali, and another
kinsman, Abu Bakr, quickly followed. Generally, however, the aristocratic clan of Abd Shams remained un-
converted and many of the first adherents to Islam
were slaves and lower class freemen.

Violent opposition to Muhammad began to develop
about A.D. 615, causing some of his followers to flee
to Abyssinia. The death of Khadija and Abu Talib,
both probably in A.D. 619, took away two powerful
protectors of the Prophet. In 620 Muhammad met
with a group of merchants primarily from the Khazraj
tribe of Yathrib and two years later he was invited to
come to that city to help settle a smoldering dispute
between the two powerful tribes, Khazraj and Aws.
Meanwhile, his enemies determined to kill Muhammad;
the Prophet escaped just in time and removed to Yathrib on July 16, 622, which later became day one of
the year one of the Moslem era.

Arriving in Yathrib (soon to be called Medina) on
September 24, A.D. 622, Muhammad immediately be-

gan to organize a resistance to Mecca. Though he suf-
fered some setbacks, Muhammad gradually increased
his power and prestige till finally in A. D. 628, under
a treaty, Muhammad led a large party of pilgrims back
to Mecca. Two years later Mecca completely surrendered to Islam and the idols were broken. The area
around the Kaaba, and by extension, the city as a
whole was declared sacred, as it remains today.

Muhammad, however, continued to rule from Medina
and gradually drew the major part of Arabia into his
orbit. At his death on June 8, 632, in Medina, he
had at least nominal control over Hejaz, Nejd, Yemen,
Oman and Hadhramaut. The death of Muhammad left
a power vacuum which was quickly filled by the appointment of Abu Bakr, who became the first Caliph
or "follower" of the Prophet.

In the century after Muhammad's death Islam had
an explosive expansion, but Arabia was at the center
of this expansion for only a short time. Under Abu
Bakr there was a period of turmoil, the Ridda or apos-
tasy, lead by a tribal leader, Musailima, of the large
Hanifa tribe. In 633, Khalid, the military genius of
Islam's founding days, defeated the Hanifa and killed
Musailima. The following year, however, saw the
death of Abu Bakr and the appointment of the second
Caliph, Omar. During the ten years of Omar's reign
(634-644) the great expansion of Islam began, Syria,
Mesopotamia, and Egypt being overrun in this period.
In 644 Omar was assassinated and another companion
of Muhammad, Othman, chosen as the third Caliph.
Othman continued to rule from Medina as had Muhammad, Abu Bakr and Omar, but field control of the far
ranging Moslem armies was already passing to commanders in Syria. Othman, who belonged to the aristocratic clan of Abd Shams, favored the Meccan aris-
tocracy, especially against Medinans. In 656 a dis-
satisfied group murdered Othman in his home at Medina.

Ali, the son of Muhammad's father's brother, Abu
Talib, and husband of Fatima, the daughter of Muhammad and Khadija, was then chosen fourth Caliph. With
Ali's election the power center temporarily moved to
Kufa on the Euphrates but on the murder of Ali in 661
a cousin of Othman, Muawiya, took power. Already
the previous year, Muawiya had been proclaimed Caliph
at Jerusalem (the third holiest city of Islam after Mecca and Medina) and he now founded the Omayyad Dynas-

ty centered at Damascus.   Arabia, geographically iso-
lated from the crossroads of world affairs, never
again became a political center of Islam, but Mecca,
where every Moslem wishes to go at least once in his
lifetime, and Medina, where the Prophet lies buried,
has guaranteed the Hejaz of Arabia a prominent place
in Islam.

The history of the peninsula since 650 has primarily
been one of domination by outside powers alternated
with (or mixed with) tribal independence.   Throughout
the later seventh century A. D. and the first half of the
eighth century the peninsula was ruled from Damascus.
In A. D. 750 the Omayyads were overthrown by the Abbasid line descendants of Al Abbas, uncle of Muhammad and a member of the Hashimite clan of the
Quraish tribe.   The Abbasids "de-Arabized" Islam and
the cultural center of power, already strongly influenced by Middle East high culture, was now Persian-
ized.   A new capital was established at Baghdad on
the Tigris.   Arabia remained under Abbasid control
though there was some local independence--for example
the Ziyadid dynasty founded by an Abbasid general Muhammad ibn Zayad in 819.   Zayad, who was sent by
the Abbasids to combat Zeidis and other Shias in Yemen, set himself up as an independent ruler.   In the
course of the ninth century A. D. other local dynasties
in the Yemen area also broke loose, as did Oman in
the southeast of the peninsula.   Around 870 an Egyptian
line of rulers, the Tulinids split off Hejaz and Asir
from the Caliphate and in 899 a revolt by the radical
Qarmatian, Shia, sect (which centered in the Hasa with
its capital at present day Hofuf) kept Islam ablaze with
internal warfare for decades.   In 930 the Qarmatians
sacked Mecca, carrying the black stone away to Hofuf
where it was kept till 951.

The tenth century was one in which numbers of con-
testing parties, Tulinids, Abbasids, Qarmatians and
various local Arab rulers struggled for control.   In
the twelfth century the Qarmatian sect still controlled
most of interior Arabia though the south was independent.   The Hejaz, however, and at least part of Asir
was overrun by the Shia Fatimid Dynasty of Egypt
around 970.   The area was under Fatimid control till
1070 when the Seljuk Turks took over parts of the
broken remnants of the old Abbasid Empire and in the
process seized the Hejaz.   Meanwhile in Egypt the Fatimid dynasty had peacefully fallen to Saladin and the

orthodox (Sunni) Ayyubid Dynasty in 1171; the Hejaz
was incorporated without problem into this new structure; and even Yemen was nominally brought under
Ayyubid rule.   It seems unlikely that either Hejaz or
Egypt had been greatly influenced by the Shia doctrines
for both accepted Sunni rule without turmoil.   This
same period saw the disappearance of the Qarmatians
as a political power.

In the mid-thirteenth century (1252) Hejaz and Asir
were overrun by another group, the slave dynasty of
Mamelukes, but the major part of the peninsula remained free and maintained tribal rule.   Shifting its
internal structure, the Mameluke power controlled the
Hejaz until 1517 when the Ottoman Turks inherited the
area.   In the Yemen, a local dynasty, the Rasulids,
originally set up by the Ayyubids, ruled from their
capital at Sana.   In 1454 they were replaced by the
Tahirids, a group dependent on the Mamelukes.   Like
the rest of Arabia, Yemen and the Hadhramaut passed
to the Ottoman Empire in the period 1519-1550.   A
further complication was the entry into Arabian waters
by the Portuguese around 1500.   The Portuguese looted
and murdered their way up the east coast of Africa
and established a foothold in the Oman area of Arabia.
The Ottoman Turks at this same time solidified their
position in the Hasa but had virtually no control over
the interior which remained in the hands of local tribal leaders.   Mecca and Medina had been ruled by local sherifs since Mameluke times and these continued,
the Meccan sherifs being members of the Hashimite
house.   After 1635 Yemen managed to re-establish virtual independence under a Zeidi group of rulers.

In the eighteenth century the Ottoman's maintained
their hold on Hejaz and on Hasa but most of the southern part of the peninsula was under control of local
rulers.   In the Nejd from about 1757 the Wahhabi
movement and the house of Saud was beginning to be
very important.   (See SAUDI ARABIA, HISTORY OF.)
The Ottomans maintained their rule (often only nominal)
over Hejaz, and Hasa in the nineteenth century, except
for an occupation of Hejaz by the Wahhabis from 1803-
1813, and reestablished a vague kind of control in Yemen.   The mid-nineteenth century saw the break up of
the first Saudi state in the Nejd.   The twentieth century has seen drastic changes--a world war that
brought about the collapse of the Ottoman Empire, and
the steady rise of the Saudi kingdom, an entity that

now controls most of the Arabian Peninsula. (See
SAUDI ARABIA, HISTORY OF.)

ARABIAN AMERICAN OIL COMPANY   see ARAMCO

ARABIAN GULF.   The body of water that extends in a north-
    west-southeast direction from the lower Mesopotamian
    lowlands to the narrows of the Straits of Hormuz which
    lead to the Gulf of Oman. All of these bodies of water
    are extensions of the Indian Ocean. Also called Per-
    sian Gulf.

ARABIAN OIL COMPANY LTD. see OIL PRODUCTION

ARABIC SCRIPT.   The second (after the Latin alphabet)
    most widely used script in today's world. The Arabic
    language is traditionally written in a cursive script of
    twenty-eight letters, each letter having an initial,
    medial and terminal form. Short vowels are normally
    not noted in Arabic writings (the Koran is an exception
    to this rule). The printed script is quite similar to
    the written one, considerably more so than in the La-
    tin alphabets. Arabic writing is from right to left
    (the numerals, however, being written from left to
    right). The Arabic alphabet is derived from the early
    Aramaic alphabet, which in turn is a descendant of an
    early North Semitic alphabet. By 700 B. C. the use of
    both Semitic Aramaic language and the associated
    script was spreading in the Syrian Iraqi area. This
    particular script spread rather widely, being utilized
    by the Nabataeans of Petra in the present-day Jordan,
    Sinai and northern Arabian area. Though the Nabata-
    ens spoke Arabic they used the Aramaic script to
    write Aramaic--their literary language. Aramaic by
    this time, around the beginning of the Christian era,
    was the most vigorous script in the Near East. At
    some point, probably in the first century A. D., the
    Nabataean variety of Aramaic script developed an off-
    shoot called Neo-Sinaitic found in the Sinai peninsula.
    This rather cursive script seems to have been the
    progenitor of the Arabic script. The latter script
    probably originated sometime in the fourth century A.
    D., the earliest physical evidence of Arabic writing
    being a trilingual (Greek-Syriac-Arabic) inscription of
    A. D. 512.
        In the early days of Islam two varieties of Arabian
    script seem to have developed, one used in the Hejaz

called Naskhi and one from Mesopotamia called Kufic
after the town Kufa, an early seat of Moslem learning.
Kufic developed into a major calligraphic style, because of the thick block-like style of its letters it lent
itself to inscriptions on stone or on metal, including
coins. The script is not used today. Naskhi, on the
other hand, a more cursive and rather elongated form
of writing, eventually became a favored script in the
Ottoman Turkish Empire and, more importantly, developed into modern Arabic writing.
The twenty-eight letters in the order used by modern
Arabic speakers are the following:

alif	(functions as	ṭa	(t)
	bearer of the hamza	ẓa	(z)
	[glottal stop] or as	'ayin	(a voiced
	lengthener of short a)		pharyngeal fricative)
ba	(b)	ghain	(gh, a voiced
ta	(t)		velar fricative)
tha	(th)	fa	(f)
jim	(j)	gaf	(k, a uvular
ha	(h)		stop)
kha	(kh)	kaf	(k, a voiceless
dal	(d)		velar stop)
dhal	(th)	lam	(l)
ra	(r)	mim	(m)
za	(z)	nun	(n)
sin	(s)	ha	(h)
shin	(sh)	waw	(w)
sad	(s)	ya	(y)
dad	(d)		

The letters alif, waw and ya are used as long vowels,
the rest always as consonants. Though not a letter in
the alphabet, the hamza, or glottal stop, is an important part of Arabic and is represented by a diacritical
mark as sometimes are the short vowels.

ARAD. Arabic name for salt bush Salsola cyclophylla that
grows on the edges of the Rub al Khali.

ARAFAT, PLAIN OF. A circular plain some twelve miles
east of the city of Mecca where pilgrims gather as
part of the pilgrimage to Mecca.

ARAFAT, STANDING ON. The climax of the pilgrimage to
Mecca which takes place on the ninth day of the month

Dhu al Hijja.   Pilgrims pray facing Mecca on this
plain till sunset.

ARAIF (The strayed camels).   Cousins of Ibn Saud who were
rescued from the Rashids at the battle of Anaiza in
1904 and restored to the Saud family.   In 1910-1912
some of these kinsmen, under Saud ibn Abdul Aziz al-
lied with the Hazzani family of the Aflaj, rebelled
against Ibn Saud, but were soundly defeated.   Saud
then linked his fortunes with Ibn Saud.

ARAMA ESCARPMENT.   A prominent physical feature of the
Nejd.   A series of Cretaceous limestone outcroppings
stretching some 500 miles in a generally north-south
direction.

ARAMCO.   The company that currently extracts Arabian oil.
The agreement between King Ibn Saud and western oil
interests was worked out in 1932 and 1933.   On May
29, 1933 the then Saudi Minister of Finance, Abdulla
Sulaiman, and the American Oil Company agent, Lloyd
N. Hamilton, signed a preliminary agreement.   In
November of 1933 assignment was made to the California Arabian Standard Oil Company (CASOC).   In 1936
the Texas Oil Company took partnership in the Arabian
contract and on January 31, 1944 title of the company
was changed to the Arabian American Oil Company or
ARAMCO.   In 1946 two other oil companies, Standard
of New Jersey and Socony-Vacuum also purchased shares
of ARAMCO.   The ARAMCO concession runs till A. D.
1999 and various parts of the concession have been re-
negotiated.
    ARAMCO's activities, within Saudi Arabia have been
marked by considerable attention to development of the
country and the company is generally regarded as a
progressive force in Arabia.
    At present the Getty Oil Company and Arabian Oil
Company (Ltd.) of Japan also have contractual agree-
ments with Saudi Arabia and Kuwait, extracting oil in
the Neutral zone between these two countries.

ARDH AS SAWWAN.   A relatively featureless desert some
seventy miles long that reaches from the Wadi Sirhan
almost to Maan, thus lying mostly in Jordan rather
than Saudi Arabia.   The Ardh as Sawwan is deeply cut
by dry wadis.

ARTAWIYA. Oasis north of Riyadh in the Nejd. Site of the
first settlement in 1912 of the Wahhabi Bedouin who,
under Ibn Saud, became the Ikhwan.

ARUNDEL, ISABEL. Wife and biographer of Sir Richard
Burton. See also BURTON, SIR RICHARD FRANCIS.

ASIR. The southwestern province of Saudi Arabia. Asir
consists of a series of highlands, actually an extension
of the highlands of Yemen. West of them is a rather
narrow coastal plain, and eastward a series of highlands that are drained by the two great wadi systems,
the Bisha and the Tathlith. The central portion of
Asir is relatively well watered with a mild climate;
the highest mountain peak in the province being some
9,400 feet. The area of Asir is 40,130 square miles
and the population is something over one million. The
region shares a northern border with the Hejaz, a
southern boundary with Yemen, and merges with Nejd
in the east and north.
　　Asir is divided into three administrative districts,
a coastal area with the capital at the seaport city of
Jizan (Qizan), an upland district with a capital at Abha,
south of Dirs at an altitude of some 7,000 feet, and
an eastern district with the capital at Khamis Mushayt
in the upper Wadi Bisha drainage.
　　In recent history Asir was controlled by the Turks
until the end of World War I. Following the war,
Asir was gradually absorbed into Saudi Arabia. The
Saudi government is presently trying to encourage agriculture in Asir. The economy at present is partly
supported by rock salt mines in the Jizan area. As
yet no significant amount of oil has been found in Asir.

ATAIBA TRIBE. Tribal group from the Hasa who, in 1783,
invaded Bahrein Island and still make up the ruling
family and most of the population of that Island. See
also BAHREIN.

ATTENE. Region mentioned by Pliny, probably at or near
present-day Hofuf.

AUSAN. Kingdom of southern Arabia in the first millenium
B.C. In its later periods, along with Qataban and
Hadhramaut this civilization was referred to as
Himyaritic rather than Minaean or Sabaean, from the
powerful tribe of Himyar.

AUXILIAIRE DE LA REGIE AUTONOME DES PETROLES
see AUXIRAP

AUXIRAP.   A French government owned company (Auxiliaire
de la Régie Autonome des Pétroles) given the authority
in an agreement signed in 1965 to prospect in the Red
Sea.

AYAINA (UYAINA).   Small town in the Wadi Hanifa near
present-day Riyadh where the religious reformer Muhammad Abdul Wahhab was born in 1703.

AYYAM AL ARAB (The days of the Arabians).   The period
of bedouin wars before the rise of Islam.   See also
ARABIA, HISTORY OF.

AZMI, NAZIH M.   A Moslem Arab from Damascus, who
visited and photographed the Dam of Marib in 1936
with a company of Yemeni soldiers.

-B-

BADANA (BADANAH).   Small city in extreme northern Saudi
Arabia which is at present a pumping station on the
Trans-Arabian Pipe Line (Tapline).

BADU.   Bedouin; also sometimes spelled BEDU.

BAHREIN (BAHRAIN).   An oil rich archipelago named for
the chief island.   Bahrein Island proper is about mid-
way between the northern portion of the peninsula of
Qatar and the Saudi Arabian mainland and partially
blocks the entryway between the Gulf of Bahrein and
the Persian Gulf proper.   The island has approximately 231 square miles of territory, the highest point being the Jabal Dukhan at some 450 feet elevation.
   The present inhabitants of Bahrein and the other islands of the group are mostly descendants of the Ataiba
tribe from the mainland of Arabia.   The ruling family
of Bahrein is drawn from this tribe.
   Oil was discovered in Bahrein in 1932 and is extracted by a British company, the Bahrein Petroleum
Company.   In 1969 Bahrein produced twenty-seven million U.S. barrels of crude oil.   The population of the
Shiekdom is approximately 200,000, mainly Shia Moslems.

BAHREIN PETROLEUM COMPANY   see BAHREIN

BALFOUR, ARTHUR JAMES, FIRST EARL OF (1848-1930).
A British statesman, who was head of the British foreign office under the Lloyd George coalition government, taking that position in December, 1916 and serving till 1919.   Balfour is mainly known, as far as
Arabian affairs are concerned, as an early architect
of the Jewish Palestinian policy.

BALSAMODENDRON MYRRHA   see MYRRH

BANDAR IBN FAISAL AL DUWISH.   Son of the Ikhwan leader of the settlement of Artawiya.   Bandar, along with
his father, was killed in the Ikhwan uprising of 1929.

BANDAR IBN TALAL.   Son of Talal, ruler of Hail who, in
1868, murdered his father's brother, Mitab, and took
the throne.   Bandar was killed in turn by another
brother of Mitab, Muhammad.   See also RASHID FAM-
ILY.

BARCHANS.   Crescent shaped sand dunes, found in the sand
deserts of Saudi Arabia.

BEDOUIN.   Nomadic peoples of the deserts of Saudi Arabia
and surrounding areas.   The Bedouins herd camels,
sheep, goats and prize riding horses.   They move
from one grazing area to another throughout the year,
though there is a great deal of variation in the movement, some Bedouin groups having oasis spots at which
they may spend long periods of the year.   There is a
great deal of social differentiation among Bedouins,
some being considered noble and pure Arab, others
having non-Arabian components.   Population estimates of
the Bedouin vary but probably less than half of the population of Saudi Arabia could be described as truly nomadic.

BEDU   see BADU, BEDOUIN

BIDA (Innovation).   The opposite of sunna, the traditions
that go back to usages of Muhammad himself.   The
term bida is also used to imply heretical ideas or interpretations.

BILAL.   The muezzin appointed by the Prophet Muhammad

who, according to Islamic tradition, was a Negro from
the Abyssinian area.

BISHA, WADI OF   see ASIR

BLACKS   see RACIAL COMPOSITION OF SAUDI ARABIA

BLOOD FEUD.   A traditional social institution in Arabia
which demanded that a man's tribe avenge his murder
either by exacting payment, or by the death of one of
the murderer's tribe.   If the latter, that death in turn
must be avenged in the same way, thus touching off a
series of killings and counter-killings that sometimes
lasted for years.

BLUNT, LADY ANNE (1837-1917).   Granddaughter of the
poet Byron and authoress of A Pilgrimage to Nejd,
Lady Anne Blunt with her husband, Wilfrid Blunt,
travelled both in Arabia and in other Near Eastern
countries.   See also BLUNT, WILFRID SCAWEN.

BLUNT, WILFRID SCAWEN (1840-1922).   British diplomat
serving in Europe and South America.   He married
Lady Anne Noel, the granddaughter of the poet Byron.
On his elder brother's death he inherited the estate of
Crabbet Park in Sussex where he established stables
for the breeding of Arabian horses.   To improve the
stables Blunt and his wife travelled in North Africa,
Asia Minor and Arabia.   He was a staunch supporter
of anti-imperialistic and nationalistic movements especially in Egypt, Ireland and India.   He wrote extensively on this subject, but perhaps he is best known
for his poetry collected in The Poetry of Wilfrid Blunt
edited by W. E. Henley and George Windham.   His
English translations of Arabic poetry are considered
very successful.

BOSWELLIA   see FRANKINCENSE

BUDGET   see SAUDI ARABIA, BUDGET OF

BULLARD, SIR READER.   British member of the 1954 arbitration board set up to settle the border dispute between Saudi Arabia and the British protectorates in the
southeast part of the peninsula.

BURAIDA.   A city in the Al Qasim district, half way be-

tween Hail and Riyadh. With its sister city, Unaiza,
about fifteen miles to the south, Buraida is on the
main network of roads leading northward to Iraq and
westward to Medina and the Hejaz. Population of Buraida is estimated at 35,000.

BURAIMI OASIS. A region between the areas of the Sulta-
nate of Muscat and Oman, the Shiekhdom of Abu Dhabi
and Saudi Arabia. In the 1940's, mainly because of
oil potential, both Saudi Arabia and the British, acting
for Muscat, Oman and Abu Dhabi, claimed the oasis.
Arbitration proceedings in 1955 broke down when the
British withdrew their member of the Arbitration Com-
mittee and occupied the area.

BURCKHARDT, JOHANN LUDWIG (John Lewis) (1784-1817).
A German educated Swiss, Burckhardt under British
sponsorship explored much of the Near East and Africa.
In 1809 Burckhardt departed for Syria where he spent
three years studying the Arabic language and Muslim
law. After gaining linguistic fluency and proficiency
interpreting law, Burckhardt went to Cairo in 1812 to
begin plans for his African explorations. While wait-
ing for the correct caravan he made an expedition up
the Nile as far as Mahass and Aswan and then into
Abyssinia, arriving in Suakim in 1814. From there
Burckhardt crossed to Jedda and made the pilgrimage
to Mecca and Medina, eventually returning to Cairo via
Yenbo. During his travels Burckhardt used the name
of Ibrahim ibn Abdulla. In 1816 and 1817 Burckhardt
was in Egypt planning an expedition to the Niger but
died from dysentery in October, 1817. During his
travels he continually sent letters and reports back to
England and some 800 volumes of manuscripts were
bequeathed to the library of Cambridge University.
His books, Travels in Arabia and Notes on the Bedouins
and Wahabys were published in 1829 and 1830 respectively.

BURTON, SIR RICHARD FRANCIS (1821-1890). A member
of an Anglo-Irish family, Burton after an irregular education, joined the 18th Regiment of Bombay Native Infantry in 1842. Burton had an excellent ear for languages and learned Gujarati, Marathi, Hindustani, Persian and Arabic. During his appointment as an assistant in the Sind survey Burton studied the customs and
rituals of Islam and in 1854 made a pilgrimage to

Mecca and Medina, a trip described in the book, A
Personal Narrative of the Pilgrimage to Al-Medinah
and Meccah, which appeared in 1855. Originally Burton had planned to travel more extensively in Arabia
but was prevented by intertribal warfare. Burton is
also well known for his travels to Somaliland, the Lake
Tanganyika region and west Africa. Burton married
Isabel Arundel in 1861. His wife shared many of his
travels and after his death in 1890 became his biographer.

-C-

CALENDAR, ISLAMIC. The Islamic calendar, unlike its
Christian counterpart, is based on the lunar year and
is 354 days long. No attempt is made to adjust this
lunar calendar to the solar year so that the twelve
months of the Moslem year rotate slowly through the
solar seasons. There is a retrogression of approximately eleven days per year from lunar to solar calendar, though, depending on the actual moon phases, it
may be ten or twelve days. This lunar calendar will
fully rotate through the solar seasons in approximately
thirty-two and one half years.
     The Moslem calendar officially begins with the
Prophet's flight from Mecca to Medina (then called
Yathrib). Caliph Omar in A. D. 637, some years after
Muhammad's death, officially fixed the beginning of the
calendar at the day the Prophet left Mecca for Medina,
July 16, A. D. 622, and this date became Muharram 1
of the Hegira year 1, or 1 A. H. [Lat., Anno Hegirae;
Arab., Anno Hijrae].
     Unlike the Christian day which begins at midnight,
the Moslem day begins at sunset, and is reckoned in
two twelve-hour periods, 6 P. M. to 6 A. M. and 6 A.
M. to 6 P. M. To use an example, 9:00 P. M. in
Christian reckoning would be 3:00 in the evening in
the Moslem hour count.
     The Islamic months, in order, are Muharram,
Safar, Rabi al Awal, Rabi al Akhir, Jumada al Aula,
Jumada al Ukhra, Rajab, Shaban, Ramadan, Shawwal,
Dhu al Qada, and Dhu al Hijja.
     As a convenience for quick rough calculation, there
is listed below the Moslem day and year for January 1
of each Christian century year from A. D. 701 and the
Christian date for Muharram 1 of each Moslem cen-

tury year to date.
                Christian year, January 1
A. D. 701 - 16 Dhu al Qada, A. H. 81
A. D. 801 - 11 Dhu al Hijja, A. H. 184
A. D. 901 - 7 Muharram, A. H. 288
A. D. 1001 - 2 Safar, A. H. 494
A. D. 1101 - 27 Safar, A. H. 494
A. D. 1201 - 23 Rabi al Awal, A. H. 597
A. D. 1301 - 19 Rabi al Akhir, A. H. 700
A. D. 1401 - 15 Jumada al Aula, A. H. 803
A. D. 1501 - 10 Jumada el Ukhra, A. H. 906
A. D. 1601 - 25 Jumada el Ukhra, A. H. 1009
A. D. 1701 - 21 Rajab, A. H. 1112
A. D. 1801 - 15 Shaban, A. H. 1215
A. D. 1901 - 10 Ramadan, A. H. 1318

                Islamic year, Muharram 1
A. H.   1 - July 16, A. D. 622
A. H. 101 - July 24, A. D. 719
A. H. 201 - July 30, A. D. 816
A. H. 301 - August 7, A. D. 913
A. H. 401 - August 15, A. D. 1010
A. H. 501 - August 22, A. D. 1107
A. H. 601 - August 29, A. D. 1204
A. H. 701 - September 6, A. D. 1301
A. H. 801 - September 13, A. D. 1398
A. H. 901 - September 21, A. D. 1495
A. H. 1001 - October 8, A. D. 1592
A. H. 1101 - October 15, A. D. 1689
A. H. 1201 - October 24, 1786
A. H. 1301 - November 2, A. D. 1883

CALIPH (Kalif or Kalifah). "Successor" to the Prophet Muhammad; the individual who succeeded to the temporal power of the Prophet. The word kalif occurs a number of times in the Koran both in singular and in the plural form kalaif, kalafa, usually in a rather general sense, referring to a group of people or to a tribe. There are two references to individuals in which the word is used, in Sad, Sura (38:27) when the person is David and in The Cow Sura (2:30) when Adam is mentioned. These passages have been used by Islamic theologians as supernatural justification for the use of this title.
    Abu Bakr, who was chosen the first caliph shortly after the Prophet's death in 632, used the term Kalif Rasul Allah (Successor of the Apostle of God). Omar

who succeeded Abu Bakr in 634 seemed to have first
used the title Successor to the Successor of the Apostle
of God but soon shortened it to a simple Caliph. Omar
also assumed the title Amir ul Muminin (Commander of
the Faithful) a title that does not occur in the Koran
but which became in later centuries a common appela-
tion for the Caliph.

The third title commonly associated with the caliphate was that of Imam which had to do with the religious function of the Caliph, the Imam being the leader
to prayer in Islamic daily public worship. The word
Imam occurs often in the Koran but with a variety of
meanings; it has been translated as leader, good example, a guide, and can be used for a book as well
as for a person.

Originally, the Caliph could, according to theory,
be any able bodied, pious adult male of the Quraish
tribe (the group to which Muhammad belonged). The
caliphate in the Quraish line was broken by the murder of the Caliph Mustasim by Hulagu in 1258. An
uncle of Mustasim, named Mustansir who escaped the
slaughter of the Abbasids in Baghdad was invested by
the Mamluk ruler of Egypt as Caliph in 1261. A line
of Caliphs continued on in Cairo for 250 years, though
with no real political power. In later centuries the
Turks, who by the fifteenth century had become the
most powerful political and military force in Islam,
took over the title. (See CALIPHATE.) By now the
original meaning of the term Caliph had become greatly changed.

CALIPHATE. The Caliph (Khalif or Khalifah) was the "Successor" of the Prophet Muhammad and the office origi-
nated from the fact that Muhammad operated in two
separate spheres. No one could replace Muhammad
in his role as Prophet for he was the final prophet.
However, Muhammad was also the political leader of
the Arabs and it was to this political role that the
term Caliph was applied. The first Caliph, Abu Bakr,
was chosen in 632 shortly after the death of Muhammad by a hastily called conclave at Medina, especially
of the leaders of the Banu Khazraj tribe. Two years
later, in 634, on the death of Abu Bakr, his successor, Omar, was chosen by a group who swore allegiance to him--in any case Omar had been a kind of
co-ruler with the aging Abu Bakr and stepped into the
Caliphate without any break. Ten years later Omar

was murdered in Medina by one Abu Lulua, a Persian Christian slave, and Othman became Caliph. The choice of Othman in 644 was not without dissention, for the group (called shura, a kind of electoral college) appointed by Omar to choose a successor were faced with two candidates, Othman and Ali, the latter a husband of Muhammad's daughter, Fatima. Othman was chosen but was killed in a revolt in 656. The plotters then offered the office to Ali.

Although Ali accepted the Caliphate, a cousin of Othman, Muawiya, governor of Syria, set himself up as rival and eventually, in 660, had himself proclaimed caliph in Jerusalem, the third most sacred city (after Mecca and Medina) of the Islamic world. The issue was decided when a dissident group, the Kharijites who had been previously defeated and scattered by Ali, attempted to assassinate both Ali and Muawiya. The latter was only slightly wounded but Ali was killed and Muawiya became the first Omayyad caliph.

The Omayyad line of caliphs lasted for almost a century during which time Islamic control spread from the Indus River to the Atlantic Ocean. The Omayyads were replaced by a rival dynasty, descendants of the Prophet's paternal uncle Abbas who, like the Omayyads, were Sunnis but who offered the non-Arab populations of the Near and Middle East more participation in state affairs. The first caliph of this Abbasid dynasty, Abul Abbas, was enthroned in 750 and carried out or permitted mass executions of his Omayyad rivals; the only important member of the family to escape was Abdul Rahman who became the founder of an Omayyad dynasty in Spain.

The Abbasid caliphate at Baghdad lasted for almost five centuries, though from 945 a Persian dynasty, the Buyits took Baghdad, seat of the Caliphate and reduced the reigning caliph and his successors to the role of figureheads.

Meanwhile a rival caliph was developing in Cairo. Members of one of the branches of the Shiite branch of Islam, those who believed in the orthodoxy of Ali, produced in 909 a Fatimid caliph. The "anti-caliphate" lasted till it was finally suppressed by Saladin in 1171, who reintroduced the name of the current Abbasid caliph in the khutba (khutbah) or Friday sermon spoken in the mosque. The days of the Abbasid caliphate were numbered however, and in 1258 the last caliph, Mustasim, was killed and Baghdad sacked by the Mon-

gol commander Hulagu.
An attempt was made to revive the Caliphate some
three years later by the Mamluk ruler of Egypt, Baybars, and an uncle of Mustasim was invested with this
office taking the name of his brother (Mustasim's father) Mustansir. This Cairo caliph soon showed evidence of ambition; Baybars withdrew support and the
Caliph was killed in an attempt to regain Baghdad.
The following year (1262) Baybars invested another Abbasid prince, Abul Abbas Ahmad, who became the
second Abbasid Caliph at Cairo. This line continued
for some two and a half centuries. Meanwhile the
name was also adopted by the Ottoman Turks who at
this time were spreading Islam to eastern Europe.
Finally, in 1517, the Sultan Salim I captured Cairo.
Popular tradition has it that the last Abbasid Caliph,
Mutawakkil, transferred the office and dignity of the
Caliphate to Salim, but this is of somewhat doubtful
historicity.

CAMBON, JULES MARTIN (1845-1935). French statesman
and Secretary-General of the Ministry of Foreign Affairs during World War I. One of the French leaders
that were determined to implement the Sykes-Picot
agreement, Cambon was especially hostile to the
British plan to place Feisal, son of Sherif Hussein of
Mecca on the throne of Syria.

CARMATHIANS see QARMATIANS

CASOC see ARAMCO

CLIMATE see ARABIA, GEOGRAPHY OF

COLLEGE OF PETROLEUM AND MINERALS AT DAHRAN.
Established by Royal Decree in September, 1963 the
college in 1970 enrolled 450 students and had a faculty
of fifty-nine members. Its budget in that year was
over four million dollars. As of 1971 the college had
three faculties: Engineering Sciences, Applied Sciences
and Pure Sciences.

COMMUNICATIONS. In the early days of the Saudi Kingdom
communications, like transportation, were no faster
than a horse or camel. The advent of radio and airplane changed this and, more recently, television has
greatly changed the communications picture in the king-

dom.   In March, 1963, a Ministry of Information was
set up to handle matters of the press and radio and
television broadcasting while the Saudi Ministry of Communications deals primarily with the postal service,
telephone and telegraph system (as well as with land,
sea and air transportation).   In 1963 the Information
budget was some 0.2% of the total Saudi budget, a
little less than a million dollars.   In the following
years the Ministry budget has doubled several times.
The 1969-1970 budget for this ministry was $21,737,540.
A great deal of the funds from the mid-1960's has gone
into television.   The Communications Ministry budget
in 1969-1970 for postal, telephone, and telegraph ser-
vice--in other words non-transportation items--was
$21,092,280.

COPPER PRODUCTION.   Although relatively little copper is
mined today in Saudi Arabia, the metal is found in the
southern plateaus area southwest of Riyadh and in the
mountains in both northern and southern Hejaz.

COSMETICS.   In Saudi Arabia certain locally produced and
also some imported items are used as cosmetics in
varying degree by both men and women.   These include antimony, ambergris, and rose water, the latter
produced in the Taif area.   In recent years manufac-
tured cosmetics from Europe, Japan and the United
States have become popular in the Kingdom.

CURZON OF KEDLESTON, GEORGE NATHANIEL, FIRST
MARQUESS (1859-1925).   British statesman, Governor
General of India from 1899 to 1905, and member of
the war cabinet during World War I, and Foreign Secretary from 1919, a post he held till 1924.   During
the period Curzon spent in the foreign office he was
much involved with the developing struggle between Ibn
Saud and the Sherif of Mecca over control of the Hejaz.

-D-

DAHHAM IBN DAWWAS.   Governor of Riyadh during the
early Wahhabi period.   Dahham was the son of a governor of Manfuha who seized power in Riyadh in a
complex struggle around 1740.   Dahham withstood the
evangelical zeal of the Wahhabi faith and the military
power of the Saud rulers of Dariya for thirty years

but finally in 1773, after the loss of his two sons,
Dawwas and Sadun, he fled leaving Riyadh to the Saudi.

DAHI   see NAFUD DAHI

DAHNA.   A tongue of red sand desert stretching over four
hundred miles from the Great Nafud of north central
Arabia (the area north of the Jabal Shammar) to the
Rub al Khali.   The Dahna is from twenty to thirty
miles wide and divides the area so important to Saudi
history, that of the central Wadi Hanifa (the Diriya and
Riyadh area) from the Persian Gulf.

DAM.   Chief town of the Wadi Dawasir oasis, population c.
3000.

DAMMAM.   The present capital of the Saudi Arabian Eastern
Province, formerly known as the Province of the Hasa.
Much of the development of Dammam has taken place
since the discovery of oil in the area and the city is a
center for Saudi oil workers.   It is also developing as
a port, and now handles most of the Persian Gulf sea
trade for Saudi Arabia.   Dammam is the eastern terminus of the Riyadh, Hofuf, Dammam railroad.   Population estimates are from 30, 000 to 35, 000 inhabitants.

DARB AL FIL.   Meaning "Road of the Elephant, " the Darb
al Fil runs from Yemen through Asir to Mecca via the
Wadi Tathlith and Wadi Tayif.   In A. D. 570, the year
of the Prophet Muhammad's birth, an Abyssinian army
accompanied by a number of elephants, marched toward
Mecca along this road and made an unsuccessful attack
on the city.

DARB ZUBAIDA.   Named after the pious wife of Caliph Ha-
run al Rashid who financed its building, Darb Zubaida
(Zubaida's Road) runs from Iraq to Mecca via Jumaima,
Hail and Medina.   All along the paved route Zubaida
built cisterns at intervals of a day's travel, about
twenty miles.   Some of the cisterns are still extensively used by the Bedouins and part of the paving stones
were used in the modern motor route.

DARIN.   Town on Tarut Island in a small enclave of the
Persian Gulf outlined in the north by the Tanura peninsula.   According to a tradition there was a Nestorian
bishopric on the island in the early seventh century

A. D. In any case the Tarut and Bahrein Island areas
and adjacent coasts were centers of early high culture.

DARIYA (Al Diriyah). The first capital of the Saudi family.
The town was settled by an ancestor of the present
Saudi family named Mani al Muraidi (or possibly by a
son of Mani named Rabia) around A. D. 1450. The new
settlement was named for another Dariya, a suburban
village of Qatif on the gulf coast. Dariya became the
center of the first Saudi Empire but was captured in
1818 by the Egyptian ruler, Muhammad Ali. The city
was ordered destroyed in June, 1819. The new Saudi
capital was then established at Riyadh a few miles
downstream in the Wadi Hanifa.

DASHT. An Arabic word meaning desert.

DATE PALM. Phoenix dactylifera, the tree that bears the
date, an important food in Arabia from early times.

DAWASIR, WADI see NEJD

D. G. SCHOFIELD. The first tanker (in 1939) to be filled
with Saudi Arabian oil. The ship was loaded at Ras
Tanura.

DHAHRAN (Dharan). City a few miles south of Dammam and
the headquarters of the ARAMCO operations in eastern
Saudi Arabia. Dhahran is the home of many of the
Company's employees. Population is some 25,000.

DHAWAHIR TRIBE. Tribal group living in the Buraimi
Oasis. The Dhawahir occupy five of the Buraimi villages, Jimi, Hili, Qattara, Mutiridh, and Ain.

DIKAKA. Areas of sand desert with sparse stands of
grasses and other plants. Much of the Nejd is covered
with this kind of vegetation.

DILAM (Ad Dilam). A settlement in the relatively water-
rich Aflaj district of east central Arabia some seventy
miles south and east of Riyadh.

DILMUN see BAHREIN

DOUGHTY, CHARLES MONTAGU (1843-1926). English explorer who travelled extensively in Arabia from 1876-

1878. Doughty's adventures in Arabia are described in the book Travels in Arabia Deserta. After his journey he devoted his life to poetry and authored the volumes Dawn in Britain and Adam Cast Forth.

DUAL MONARCHY. The period between 1927 and 1932 during which time King Ibn Saud ruled over a dual Kingdom of Hejaz and Nejd. On September 18, 1932 a unified kingdom of Saudi Arabia was formed.

DUKHAN, JABAL   see BAHREIN

DUNUM. A measure used in Saudi Arabia equal to 1,000 square meters.

-E-

EASTERN AND GENERAL SYNDICATE. The British oil company to which Ibn Saud granted oil concessions in 1923. The company allowed the concession to lapse when it was decided that the chances of finding oil in Saudi Arabia were poor.

EASTERN PROVINCE OF SAUDI ARABIA. This province, originally called the Province of Hasa, is now the center of oil production in the kingdom. The capital city is Dammam, and other important centers include Khobar, Dhahran, and Hofuf, the old capital. See also HASA.

EDUCATION. In post World War II years the Saudi Arabian government has spent a considerable amount of its large income on schools. In the year 1969-1970 approximately $130,000,000 was allotted to education, more than triple the amount spent ten years before. The older Directorate General of Education was, in 1954, lifted to a full ministry. As of 1969 the Kingdom was divided into twenty-three educational districts each with a certain amount of autonomy in planning and projects under overall guidelines of the ministries.

Schools and Students in the Kingdom

	No. of Schools	No. of Students
Primary Schools (1968)	1472	342, 596
Night Schools (offering four year's courses for adults, 1968)	550	34, 824
Intermediate Schools (1968)	150	30, 716
Secondary Schools Pre-college (1968)	14	4, 949
Preparatory for College of Sharia and Islamic Studies (1968)	30	5, 834
Commercial Schools (1966)	4	960
Agricultural Schools (1966)	5	844
Industrial Schools (1965)	8	2, 414
Special Education Schools (for handicapped) (1970)	10	1, 132
Private Schools (all levels) (1968)	76	17, 040
Colleges		
Petroleum and Minerals, Dhahran (1970)		450
Sharia College, Mecca (1970)		313
College Education, Mecca (1970)		415
Sharia College, Riyadh (1968)		753
Arabic Language, Riyadh (1968)		617
Universities		
Riyadh (1970)		2, 899
Islamic at Medina (1967)		764
National King Abdul Aziz University (Private) Jedda (1970)		265

At present some 100, 000 girls and more than 250, 000 boys are involved in primary education. Education including university training, is free.

EMIR. The Arabic title meaning commander or leader, sometimes used to denote a prince.

EMPTY QUARTER see RUB AL KHALI

ERYTHRAEAN PERIPLUS.   An account written around A. D.
    200 by an unknown Greek sea captain or merchant,
    probably from Alexandria.   The Periplus includes a
    considerable amount of information on Arabia.   On the
    northern end of the Red Sea, perhaps somewhere near
    modern Dhaba south of the Gulf of Aqaba was the harbor
    of Leuke Kome (White Town) from which a caravan road
    ran to Petra.   At this time there was a Roman garri-
    son at Leuke Kome.   Further south, perhaps near the
    modern town of Mocha, was the important market cen-
    ter of Musa, controlled by Arabs but with a Roman
    trading colony.   Still further south at the site of Ocelis,
    somewhere near modern Turba, was an anchorage con-
    trolled by the king of Musa.   At Eudaemon (Aden) there
    was a superior stopping place but this was destroyed a
    few years before the Periplus was written, probably by
    the king of Musa.
        The Periplus also mentions the King of Sabratha in
    the Hadhramaut who was involved in a rich trade of
    precious metals, cloth and horses.   The island of Dis-
    coride (Socotra) was an entrepôt for trade with India.
    Farther east was the port of Moscha in the Dhufar area
    east of present-day Salala that in the days of the Peri-
    plus seems to have been part of the kingdom of Hadhra-
    maut.   This was a center for frankincense and in fact,
    the Dhufar region has optimal climatic conditions for
    this tree.
        Still farther east was an area under Persian rule,
    probably identified with modern Oman.   The Periplus
    also describes ports in the Persian Gulf, one of which,
    Ommana, was perhaps located in present-day north-east
    Saudi Arabia.

ERYTHRAEAN SEA.   Greco-Roman name for the Red Sea
    and for parts of the Indian Ocean.

EUTING, JULIUS.   A German archaeologist who travelled
    with Charles Huber in 1883 through the Jabal Shammar.

-F-

FAISAL AL DUWISH.   Member of the Mutair tribe and chief
    of the Ikhwan city of Artawiya.   In the war against the
    Ikhwan of 1929, Faisal and his son Bandar were both
    killed in the battle of the Plain of Sibila.

FAISAL IBN TURKI IBN SAUD. Son of Turki ibn Abdulla
which latter ruler, after restoring the Saudi fortunes
in the period c. 1820-1834, had been assassinated in
the latter year. Faisal revenged his father by killing
the assassin and managed to maintain Saudi rule in
Nejd in part with the help of Abdulla ibn Rashid, ruler
of the Jamal Shammar whose capital was at Hail. The
death of Faisal in 1865 led to a complicated situation
where two sons of Faisal, Abdulla and Saud struggled
for power. This struggle allowed the Rashids to inter-
fere more and more with the politics in the Wadi Hanifa.

FAISAL, KING OF SAUDI ARABIA. Faisal ibn Abdul Aziz
ibn Abdul Rahman al Faisal al Saud was born in the
late fall of 1906 (in the month of Shawwal 1324 A.H.),
the fourth son of Abdul Aziz Ibn Saud and the first
born in the recently recaptured Saudi capital of Riyadh.
Faisal's mother was Tarfa, a daughter of the Al ash
Sheik family. There were three brothers who had been
born before the Saud family reestablished themselves at
Riyadh, Turki (who died in 1918), Saud, and Khalid,
who died as a boy. Faisal's mother was a member of
the family of Muhammad ibn Abdul Wahhab, the famous
reformer and founder of Wahhabism. In childhood Faisal was to receive religious instruction from his ma-
ternal grandfather, Sheik Abdulla ibn Abdul Latif al
Sheik.
     Although in his mid-teens, Faisal was sent to Lon-
don and Paris to aid on post-World War I negotiations,
though actual control of the talks was in the hands of
an older man, Ahmad al Thunayan. It was on this
trip (in a courtesy note from Faisal to Lord Montagu,
British Secretary of State for India) that the title of
King for Ibn Saud seems to have been first used.
     In 1921 Faisal was placed in command of an expedi-
tion to Asir by King Ibn Saud. Faisal's skill as tacti-
cian and his leadership abilities led to a Saudi victory.
In 1924 a similar expedition, after the Aidh family of
highland Asir rebelled against the Saudi government,
was also completely successful.
     In 1925 following the successful Saudi conquest of
the Hejaz, Faisal became the Viceroy of that part of
Arabia. He was also made Foreign Minister of the
kingdoms, logically enough because of his travels
abroad. In 1933-1934 Faisal again was involved with
the Southern Arabian area, leading the victorious Saudi

armies in that year against Yemen.
During the Second World War Faisal represented the
interests of Saudi Arabia abroad, spending a considerable amount of time in the United States. He was one
of the architects of the United Nations and was in San
Francisco for the founding of the body.
In 1953 King Ibn Saud died and Faisal's older brother,
Saud ibn Abdul Aziz ibn Abdul Rahman Al Saud, took
the throne. Saud had been viceroy of the Nejd and
from 1953 President of the Council Ministers. In 1954
Faisal was made President of the Council of Ministers
and gradually became more and more active in the
power structure of Saudi Arabia. In 1958 Faisal was
given extraordinary powers by his brother, the king, to
solve the serious financial crisis of the state. He resigned in 1960, relinquishing the executive powers he
had been ceded by Saud. However in November of 1962
Faisal was reinstated and in March of 1964 was given
essentially the full executive power of the State, since
Saud during this period was suffering from serious ill-
nesses. Finally on November 2, 1964 Faisal was for-
mally invested with the title of King.
Faisal's rule in Arabia has been marked with a
series of basic reforms, social, administrative and
financial. Social reforms included the abolishment of
slavery, and achievement of financial stability. The
Saudi riyal since the mid 1960's has been an influen-
cial currency, widely used in the peninsula outside of
Saudi Arabia. Faisal's political and administrative reforms include a considerable reorganization of the central government. Faisal has been especially interested
in agriculture and in water availability, experimenting
with the reclamation of sea water as well as extending
the search (begun by his father) for pools of fossil
water. He has encouraged education; although the University of Riyadh was founded under King Saud, it has
grown most rapidly during the period when Faisal was
in control of the government.
Faisal has also continued a considerable and active
foreign policy, visiting a number of the Asiatic and
African Moslem states, both Arab and non-Arab. During the Arab-Israeli war of 1967 King Faisal joined
with the other Arab states but at the end of the war
influenced the other oil producing powers to resume
oil shipments to the west. One very thorny problem
(still unsettled as of 1972) is that of Yemen. In 1967
Faisal and Nassar of Egypt made a tentative settlement
of the Yemen problem but the situation still remains

rather confused and unstable.

FAISALI SCHOOL.   Term sometimes used for the political
and social philosophy of King Faisal.   This is essentially a plan of gradual social reform and economic ad-
vancement developed strictly within the perimeters of
the Sharia.   The program of King Faisal as it devolves
in the 1960's and early 1970's is one of gradualism,
with considerable attention paid to matters of education
and health but with a balance of state and private capi-
talism.   Economic goals of the system as far as individuals are concerned are for the kinds of protection
and guarantees, against unemployment, illness, disa-
bility and old age that are perhaps more characteristic
of Western European mixed-economy democracies rather than of the Communist bloc.   The Faisal philosophy
differs from that of the west in having a virtual identity
of church and state, and lack of development of consti-
tutional democracy.

FARASAN ISLANDS.   A group of low-lying islands about ten
miles off the southern coast of Asir, directly across
from the port city of Jizan.   The islands are made up
mainly of salt domes and have some economic value as
salt producers.

FARTAK, CAPE OF (Ras Fartak).   Cape of land in western
Hadhramaut, presently a part of the Peoples Republic
of South Yemen.

FAUNA   see ARABIA, FAUNA OF

FETWA.   A canonical ruling by the Ulema.

FIRST HEGIRA.   The flight of certain of the poorer and
more vunerable converts of Muhammad to Christian
Abyssinia to escape persecution by the people of Mecca.   This flight took place c. A.D. 613.
  According to some accounts eighty-three people fled
to Abyssinia including Othman of the Omayya clan who
later became third Caliph and ancestor of the Omayyad
dynasty.

FIVE PILLARS OF FAITH.   The acts of faith that every
good Moslem must accept.   These include the profession of faith, prayer, almsgiving, fasting, and pilgrimage.   See also ISLAM.

FLAG   see SAUDI ARABIA, FLAG OF

FLORA   see ARABIA, FLORA OF

FRANKINCENSE.   The aromatic resin of the genera Boswellia.   There are two major varieties, the Boswellia
sacra, which is bush in form, growing to eight to ten
feet in height without a central trunk.   The Boswellia
carterii on the other hand has a central trunk.   The
frankincense plant has spreading branches and red
flowers.   The resin is pale yellow to green and yellow-
brown and is translucent when first gathered.   It is
collected by cutting and peeling the bark of the tree in
short strips.   This is done in the summer; in the fall
the hardened globules of resin are collected.   When
burned in a smoldering or reducing atmosphere it has
a distinctive and pleasant aroma.
    Frankincense was traded from southern Arabia to
the Mediterranean world from Egyptian Old Kingdom
days on.   It was widely used in religious ceremonies
by the various Mediterranean peoples and by such
groups to the east as the Persians.   In Greco-Roman
times it was widely used to disguise the odor of burn-
ing bodies during cremations.   The center of frankincense growth is in the Hadhramaut, especially at altitudes of about 2,000 feet.   The only other area in
which the plant occurs naturally is Somaliland.

FUJAIRAH.   One of the Trucial Coast states that, in 1971,
joined the Union of Arab Emirates.   See also TRUCIAL
COAST.

                            -G-

GALLUS, AELIUS.   Roman Prefect of Egypt who, in 24 B.C.
made an attack on the area of Yemen.   Aelius marched
down the Hejaz, the range of hills that runs down the
western side of Arabia, paralleling the Red Sea.   Utilizing Nabataean guides, the Roman army reached as
far south as the Wadi Najran at about the present Saudi
Arabia-Yemen border.   From that point the Romans,
for some reason or other, retreated (the records are
not entirely clear as to what happened but supplies or
water may have run short).   At any rate this represented the high point of Roman penetration into southern
Arabia and the Himyarite kingdom of Yemen based on
Marab escaped Roman rule.

GENERAL PETROLEUM AND MINERAL AUTHORITY see PETROMIN

GEOGRAPHY see ARABIA, GEOGRAPHY OF

GEOLOGY see ARABIA, GEOLOGY OF

GERRA. A city, or perhaps territory, located in the present Hasa with its seaport at or near the present town of Uqair east of Hofuf. Gerra, in Greco-Roman times, seems to have been engaged as middleman in a trade network that extended from India to the Mediterranean world.

GETTY OIL COMPANY see OIL PRODUCTION

GHATGHAT. One of the very earliest of the Ikhwan settlements. Ghatghat is located south of Dhurma and some thirty miles west of Riyadh.

GHAWAR. An oil field in the Hasa west of Abqaiq. The Arabic word ghawar refers to erosion-formed caves and rock shelters, a feature of the area.

GHAWARA MINE see GOLD PRODUCTION

GHAZU. The traditional practice in Arabia of minor raiding. Ghazu is thought of somewhat as a sport and usually ends by an agreement to finish the "contest" at a later date. Raiding, however, was practically eliminated by Ibn Saud.

GHURAIMIL. A hill south of Abqaiq where in the winter of 1789-1790 the Saudi state under Abdul Aziz I Ibn Saud defeated the powerful Banu Khalid, ruling tribe of the Hasa.

GHUSIBA see LEILA

GHUTRA see KAFFIYEH

GINDIBU THE ARABIAN. A ruler, presumably from somewhere in the Arabian peninsula, who sent a thousand camels (no doubt with riders) to aid a confederacy of Syrian states at the Battle of Karkar (854 or 853 B.C.) against the Assyrian king Shalmaneser III.

GLASER, VON EDUARD. First European to visit the famous
Dam of Marib in 1888, a number of other Europeans
having failed in the attempt. Glaser spent a month in
the area in Arab disguise, at considerable risk to himself.

GOLD PRODUCTION IN SAUDI ARABIA. There are a number of gold producing areas in Saudi Arabia, the most
important being the Mahab Dhahab region between Mecca and Medina, the Ammar mine some 125 miles south
and west of Riyadh (west of the Tuwaiq Escarpment),
the Ghawara mine a few miles further south and west,
and Aqiq Ghamid mines some 125 miles south-east of
Mecca. See also MAHAD DHAHAB and SAUDI ARABI-
AN MINING SYNDICATE LTD.

GOODWILL MISSION FROM AMERICA. Financed by the
Emergency Fund of the President of the United States,
K. S. Twitchell, J. G. Hamilton, and A. L. Walthen
were sent to Saudi Arabia in 1942 on a goodwill mission from the State Department. The purpose of the
mission was to examine agricultural possibilities and
make recommendations on methods of developing Saudi
Arabian agriculture.

GRAND MUFTI. In Saudi Arabia, chief expounder of Islamic
law and head of the Ulema.

GREAT NAFUD. The northern desert area of Arabia, approximately 22,000 square miles, lying to the east of
Mt. Sharr and Mt. Loz. This region receives some
winter rains from the Mediterranean and has a short
but intense growing season that has considerable economic implications for the inhabitants.

-H-

HADA see TAIF

HADD, CAPE OF (RAS HADD). The easternmost extension
of Arabia at the mouth of the Gulf of Oman.

HADDA AGREEMENT. An agreement in 1922 that fixed the
boundary between Saudi Arabia and what was, then, the
British controlled state of Transjordan.

HADHAN, MOUNTAIN OF. Mountain peak in the vicinity of
    Taif.

HADHRAMAUT. The district on the south coast of Arabia
    bounded on the west by Yemen, on the east by Oman
    and on the north by Saudi Arabia. Hadhramaut was,
    in antiquity, one of the sources for the famous myrrh
    and frankincense. It was in pre-Islamic times the cen-
    ter of a considerable civilization. At present Hadhra-
    maut is included in the Peoples Republic of Southern
    Yemen.

HADITH. The narrative or "statements" of Sunna, which in
    turn are usages, prescriptions, prohibitions, or any
    kind of instruction set down by Muhammad or actions
    inferred from his example. These statements were
    used interpreting and supplementing the Koran and vast
    numbers of them were collected in the early centuries
    of Islam. They were validated by a chain of authori-
    ties going back to Muhammad himself or to one of his
    companions who had opportunity to observe the behavior
    of the Prophet. The common method of validation is
    to use a formula such as "X told me that Y told him
    a story heard from Z, a companion of the Prophet who
    had it from the Prophet."
        Two very important collections of Hadith were made
    by Al Bukhari (810-870) and by Muslim (817-875), each
    with the title of Al Sahih (the genuine). Bukhari's work
    especially had tremendous impact on the Islamic world
    and is generally regarded today as second only to the
    Koran as a religious text. Bukhari is said to have
    examined some hundreds of thousands of Hadith of
    which he extracted 2762 as authentic. Bukhari's work
    is contained in 97 sections (each devoted to some gene-
    ral subject) of 3450 chapters. The work is one of very
    careful and detailed scholarship. There is no complete
    translation of Al Sahih into English, though selections
    have been made. A complete translation in French,
    however, has been made by O. Houdas and W. Mar-
    cais.
        Other collections of Hadith were also made during
    this same period. They include the Kitab as-Sunan of
    Abu Daud (817-888), the Jami as-Sahih of Tirmidhi (?-
    892), the Kitab as-Sunan of Nasai (830-915), and the
    Kitab as-Sunan of Ibn Maja (824-866).

HAIL. The chief city of the Jabal Shammar district of

northern Saudi Arabia. Hail was, in the nineteenth and
early twentieth centuries, the capital of the Rashid family who until 1902 controlled much of the northern Nejd,
including Riyadh itself. Hail has a population estimated
at 20,000 to 25,000.

HAJAR MOUNTAINS. A mountain chain in Oman that roughly parallels the Gulf of Oman. Individual peaks extend
to 10,000 feet.

HAJJ. The Pilgrimage to Mecca which every Moslem should
make at least once in a lifetime.

HAJJI. The honorific given a person who has completed the
Hajj or Pilgrimage to Mecca.

HALALAH. A small unit of currency, since 1960 one fifth
of a qirsh and one hundredth of a Saudi Arabian riyal.

HALEVY, JOSEPH. Nineteenth century explorer in the
southern Arabian peninsula, Halevy visited Marib, Jauf,
the Rub al Khali, and Najran during the period from
1869-70.

HAMILTON, LLOYD N. see ARAMCO

HAMUD IBN SUBHAN. Member of an influential family in
Hail who helped in restoring the rightful Rashidi heir,
Saud ibn Abdul Aziz, in 1909. Hamud became regent
for the ten year old Saud. He was poisoned a few
months after accepting this office and his brother Zamil succeeded him.

HAMUR. Local name for a Persian Coast grouper that lives
near the shore, often under rock ledges. The hamur,
which is used for food, may weight as much as thirty
pounds.

HANAFI. One of the four schools of jurisprudence that appeared in orthodox or Sunni Islam in the eighth and
ninth centuries A.D., named for its founder Abu Hanifa
of Iraq who died A.D. 776. The adherents of Hanafi
depended strongly on analogy in the interpretation of
the Koran. Hanafi interpretations are common today
in the area of the old Ottoman Empire. Hanafi is the
only major sect of Islam that permits prayers to be
said in languages other than Arabic.

HANBALI. Named for a ninth century scholar, Ahmad Ibn
     Hanbal (died 855), Hanbali is one of the four schools of
     jurisprudence that appeared in Sunni Islam in the eighth
     and ninth centuries A.D. Hanbal and a fellow theolo-
     gian, Daud al Zahiri (died 883), took a strongly tradi-
     tionalist viewpoint. Hanbal was a student of Shafi but
     disagreed with his teacher on a number of points, es-
     pecially on the validity of points of laws formulated by
     boards of religious scholars. He led a kind of "back
     to the Koran" movement a bit like the evangelical
     movements that swept Christian society in early modern
     times. The Hanbali school had considerable success
     especially in Iraq and Syria until the Turkish period.
     In the eighteenth century it was revived by Muhammad
     ibn Abdul Wahhab under the name Wahhabism in the
     Nejd of north central Arabia and is today the preferred
     sect of Saudi Arabia.

HANIF. A little known group in the Arabia of immediately
     pre-Islamic times who, influenced by Christians and
     Jews, were developing monotheistic ideas. Cousins of
     both the Prophet Muhammad and of his first wife
     Khadija were supposed to have been Hanifs. The ex-
     tent of Hanif influence is not clear.

HANIFA, WADI see NEJD

HARAM see MECCA

HARAN. A small oasis city some 150 miles southeast of
     Riyadh in the Jafura district and a point on the Riyadh
     to Qatif-Dhahran railroad. In 1964 Haran became a
     focus for the Al Faisal agricultural settlement which
     aimed at resettling some 8000 Bedouins as farmers.
     The Project was completed in 1971 and involved the
     distribution of 40,000 acres of land with water supplied
     by deep (up to 670 feet) wells. Dates, grain and vege-
     tables are produced at this new area.

HARIM [HAREM]. Traditionally, separate quarters of the
     women, into which only men of close family connections
     are allowed to enter. There are no mixed social
     gatherings and women appear in public heavily veiled.
     The policy of educating girls and the general impact
     of westernization in Saudi Arabia, are slowly changing
     these practices.

HARIQ OASIS.   An oasis area in the Tuwaiq Mountains south
    of Riyadh.

HARM.   Green salt bush that grows in parts of the Rub al
    Khali.   Zygophyllum sp.

HARRA.   The region of lava in the northern Hejaz, east of
    the coastal range, which makes communications with
    the interior of northern Arabia difficult.

HARRAT.   Arabic word for lava fields.

HASA.   The Hasa region, now known as the Eastern Pro-
    vince of Saudi Arabia.   Lying between the Dahna and
    the waters of the Persian Gulf, Hasa has long been
    famous for its large number of springs and oases.
    Since the late 1930's it has become the center of Saudi
    Arabian oil production.
        Historically, the capital of Hasa has been at Hofuf,
    the center of Qarmatian power in the tenth and eleventh
    A.D. centuries.   In 1953 the capital of the new Eastern
    Province was moved to Dammam near Dhahran.

HASA, OASIS OF.   A dominant feature of the old Province
    of the Hasa, this oasis is the largest in Saudi Arabia.
    There are some sixty springs, four of them extremely
    large.   The area has been known for a very long time;
    Hofuf, the main city, seems to date at least to Greco-
    Roman times.

HASHIM.   Father of Abdul Mutallib whose son, Abdullah,
    was, in turn, the father of Muhammad.   Hashim was
    from the Meccan tribe of Quraish but married a woman
    from the Adi ibn al Najjar clan of the Khazraj tribe of
    Medina.   This connection with Medina was to be of
    great importance to the Prophet in the early years of
    his ministry.

HAUTA, OASIS OF.   An oasis and settlement in central Nejd
    on the line of the Jabal Tuwiaq south of Riyadh.

HAWR.   Arabic word for lake.

HEALTH SERVICES AND MEDICINE.   Since the Second World
    War Saudi Arabia has put considerable emphasis on
    health care and delivery.   The Ministry of Health in
    1969-70 had a budget of some thirty-seven million dol-

lars (some five dollars per capita). In 1970 there were forty-nine hospitals in the kingdom, 6299 hospital beds, 180 health clinics and 271 health units. In 1969 the nation had the following number of medical and paramedical personnel:

Physicians	737
Dentists	33
Pharmacists	50
Male nurses	1385
Nurses, midwives and assistants	672
Pharmacy assistants	447
Laboratory assistants	184
X-ray assistants	98

HEGIRA. The journey of the Prophet Muhammad from Mecca to the oasis town of Yathrib (later called Medina) some 300 miles to the north. The Hegira began on July 16, A.D. 622, and Muhammad reached Yathrib-Medina on September 24, A.D. 622. The former date, a few years later, was officially proclaimed as the first day of the first year of the Islamic era.

HEGIRA, FIRST see FIRST HEGIRA

HEJAZ. The area of highlands and narrow sea coast in north-western Arabia that was the cradle of Islam. At present Hejaz is one of the five major provinces or subdivisions of Saudi Arabia following its capture by King Ibn Saud in 1925. On January, 1926, Ibn Saud took the title of King of Hejaz, the Kingdom of Saudi Arabia itself being formed in 1932. Before the Saudi period, the Hejaz had been nominally under Turkish rule (until the end of World War I) but much control was invested in the Hashimite Sherifs of Mecca.

The area of the Province of the Hejaz is approximately 134, 600 miles and has a population of some two million. The northern boundary of Hejaz is shared with Jordan while the southern boundary with Asir is the line of the Wadi Amq. The boundary with Nejd is not well defined.

Major cities of Hejaz include the two great religious centers of Mecca and Medina. The port city of Jedda is one of the seats of government of Saudi Arabia, containing foreign embassies and the Saudi Foreign Office. Jedda also serves as port for pilgrimages to Mecca and Medina, the city being now connected to both these centers with paved roads. Pilgrims going to Medina

can also disembark at the port of Yenbo north of Jedda.
Another important town in the Hejaz is Taif, which is
to the east of Mecca and, at 5500 feet, at considerable
higher altitude.   Taif has long served as a kind of
summer capital for the province, and to some degree
of the nation as a whole.
     Good roads today link Jedda with Mecca, Medina,
Taif, and Riyadh in the Nejd.   In the period 1904 to
1908 a railroad was built by the Turks from Damascus
and Maan to Medina but this was destroyed in the First
World War.   (See HEJAZ RAILROAD below.)

HEJAZ RAILROAD.   A railway built by the Turks with Ger-
     man engineers connecting Maan in Jordan with Medina.
     The road reached Medina in 1908, but a proposed ex-
     tension to Mecca was never completed.   Its purpose
     was to provide transportation for pilgrims to Mecca
     and, incidentally for Turkish troops in the event of war.
     T. E. Lawrence and his guerilla troops destroyed the
     railway during World War I.   Sections of the railroad
     were used after the war but it was eventually deserted.

HIJAZ   see HEJAZ

HIJIRA   see HEGIRA

HIMYARITIC CIVILIZATION.   The name by which the civili-
     zations of Ausan, Qataban and Hadhramaut were known
     in their later period.   Called Himyaritic, rather than
     Minean or Sabaean, this culture was named after the
     powerful tribe of Himyar.

HODEIDA.   The chief port of Yemen on the Red Sea west
     and slightly south of Sana.   Hodeida is connected to
     Sana by a major highway.

HOFUF.   The former capital of the Saudi Arabian Eastern
     Province (the Province of the Hasa).   Hofuf was, in the
     tenth and eleventh centuries, the capital of the Shia ex-
     tremist group, the Qarmatians.   In 1871 the city became
     the administrative center for Turkish rule in eastern
     Arabia.   In 1913 the city was captured by Ibn Saud and
     incorporated into what was to become the Saudi Kingdom.
     A point of interest in Hofuf is the nineteenth century
     mosque of Ibrahim Pasha.   The population is something
     over 100,000.

HOGARTH, DAVID GEORGE (1862-1927). A British arche-
ologist and intelligence agent. The son of a clergyman,
Hogarth became keeper of the Ashmolean Museum in
1909, a post he held till his death. Hogarth seems to
have recruited T. E. Lawrence into the intelligence
service even before World War I. During that War,
in 1915 Hogarth was sent to Cairo to help organize an
Arab revolt against the Turks in the Middle East. He
quickly built up the Arab Bureau and had a hand in the
contacts between Lawrence and the Sherif of Mecca.
After the war Hogarth was British Commissioner at the
Middle East Commission section of the Paris peace
conference.

HOLMES, MAJOR FRANK. An engineer from New Zealand,
Holmes went to Bahrein in the early 1920's to help
develop water resources. His main interest, however,
seems to have been oil, and in 1922 he crossed into
Saudi Arabia to gain a concession in the Hasa from Ibn
Saud. In 1923 a concession for more than 30,000
square miles was granted to the British group that
Holmes represented, the Eastern and General Syndicate.
Two years later Holmes obtained a concession in Bahrein for his company. The Hasa concession was allowed
to lapse and Gulf Oil Corporation of the United States
took over the option in 1927.

HORMUZ, STRAIT OF. Straits between southern Iran and
eastern Arabia that separate the Arabian or Persian
Gulf from the Gulf of Oman.

HUBAL. The chief deity of the Kaaba in Mecca in pre-Islamic times. Hubal seems to have been represented
as a crude human figure. The idol was destroyed
with others at the final victory of Islam following the
Hegira.

HUBER, CHARLES. One of the first Europeans to cross the
Nefud. His travels were recorded in Journal d'un
Voyage en Arabie, 1883-1884.

HUFUF   see HOFUF

HURGRONJE, SNOUCK (1855-1936). A Dutch scholar who
travelled extensively in the Arabian peninsula in the
late nineteenth century. Hurgronje became a Moslem
and visited Mecca, the subject of one of his books.

IBN DIRA. Cousin of Mani al Muraidi, a founder of the
Saud Dynasty. In 1446 Mani went from his home near
Al Qatif, a town on the Persian Gulf north and west of
Bahrein Island, to visit Ibn Dura who was living at
Manfuha near Riyadh in north central Arabia. As a
result of this visit either Mani or his son Rabia was
given land on the, then, relatively deserted Wadi Hani-
fa. Rabia with fellow settlers from their home in
Dariya near Qatif founded the new Dariya in the Wadi
Hanifa. This city soon became a rising and aggressive
power in the central part of the Arabian peninsula.

IBN HISHAM. Died A.D. 833. Editor of the earlier Sirah
or life of the Prophet Muhammad written by Ibn Ishaq.

IBN ISHAQ. Died A.D. 768, the composer of the first life
of the Prophet Muhammad that has come down to us.
His Sirah has been preserved in a later edition, that
of Ibn Hisham.

IBN JILUWI. A cousin of Ibn Saud who, in the 1902 Saudi
attack against Riyadh, killed the Rashidi governor,
Ajlan.

IBN SAAD. Died A.D. 845. Secretary of Al Wiqidi and the
compiler of the Tabaqat, biographies of the companions
of the Prophet Muhammad.

IBN SAUD, KING AND FOUNDER OF SAUDI ARABIA. Full
name Abdul Aziz ibn Abdul Rahman al Faisal al Saud,
or, sometimes, in the regal years Abdul Aziz II ibn
Saud, of the Faisal branch of the great Saudi house.
Ibn Saud was born in Riyadh, probably in 1880--one
date often given is 22 Dhu al Hijja 1297 A.H. or November 26, A.D. 1880. He was a fourth child, having
two older brothers Faisal and Fadh and an older sister, Nura. His mother was Sara bint Sudairi of the
Wadi Dawasir region.
    At the time of Ibn Saud's birth, Abdul Rahman was
engaged in a desperate struggle with the Rashidi house
of the Shammar tribe whose capital at Hail (Hayal) lies
some 300 miles to the northwest of Riyadh on the edge
of the Great Nafud. The struggle went badly for Abdul
Rahman and in January of 1891 the Saudi family was
forced to flee Riyadh. Abdul Rahman moved first to

Bahrein Island, at that time under British protection,
where young Abdul Aziz was treated for rheumatic fe-
ver.   On recovery, the boy settled for a time among
the Banu Murra, a Bedouin tribe in the northern Rub
al Khali, and there learned nomadic Bedouin ways.
After a stay with the Murra tribe, Abdul Rahman
settled in the coastal town of Kuwait.   He made brief
visits to the Hasa, where the Turks had recently reestablished themselves but refused offers of Turkish
help in regaining Riyadh.   In any event, young Ibn Saud,
himself, took the town by surprise attack in January,
1902 with a small group of followers.   From that date
began the rise in fortunes that was to lead to the Kingdom of Saudi Arabia.

The first years after reestablishment of Saudi rule
were spent in a complex struggle with the Rashids and
political maneuverings with the British who controlled
Kuwait, the Turks of the Hasa, and the Hashimite
sheiks of the Hejaz.   It was during this period that Ibn
Saud began settlements of Ikhwan (Brotherhood), Bedouin Wahhabis who were settled as para-military
groups in agricultural towns.

After the First World War removed the Turkish influence from Arabia and generally upset the balance of
power, Ibn Saud rapidly overran the pro-Turkish Rashids, completing the conquest of their territory in
1922.   He then turned westward to the Hejaz where the
British (partly due to the influence of Lawrence of
Arabia) backed the Hashimite sheikh, Hussein.   This
war was marked by a massacre by fanatical Ikhwan at
Taif east of Mecca.   In 1926 conquest of the Hejaz was
completed.   In 1927 a dual kingdom of Hejaz and Nejd
was organized and on September 18, 1932, by royal decree; this dual monarchy was united in the Kingdom of
Saudi Arabia.

In the early 1930's Ibn Saud added Asir to his kingdom of Saudi Arabia and defeated Yemen--choosing,
perhaps for administrative reasons, to leave that country independent.

Perhaps the most notable economic event of Ibn
Saud's career took place in 1933 when the King signed
a sixty-six year oil lease agreement with the company
later known as ARAMCO (q.v.).   Though not immediately successful, the company, by World War II, was
pouring money into Arabian coffers and in post-war
years oil revenues have been responsible for Saudi
Arabia's modernization program.

Following the Yemen war Ibn Saud became a major force for peace in the Near East and an important influence for Arab unity. In World War II the King was officially neutral. King Ibn Saud died at Taif on November 9, 1953.

IBRAHIM. A son of Muhammad borne by a Coptic Christian named Mariya (Mary), who had been given to Muhammad as a concubine around A.D. 628. She seems to have outlived the Prophet, but Ibrahim died in infancy to the great sorrow of his father.

IBRAHIM AGA. Arabic name of Thomas Keith, governor of Medina in 1815. See also KEITH, THOMAS.

IBRAHIM IBN ABDULLA. Arab name of Johann Ludwig Burckhardt. See also BURCKHARDT, JOHN LUDWIG.

IBRAHIM PASHA. Son of Muhammad Ali, early nineteenth century ruler of Egypt under the Ottoman Turks. Ibrahim was in command of the Egyptian army that captured the Saudi capital of Dariya in September, 1818.

ID AL ADHHA. The Feast of the Sacrifice, a major Sunni celebration and one of two official national religious holidays in Saudi Arabia. This celebration begins on the tenth day of the twelfth Islamic month, Dhu al Hijja, and lasts four days. In 1971 the tenth of Dhu al Hijja (A.H. 1390) fell on February 6.

ID AL FITR. The feast, one of the two national religious holidays in Saudi Arabia, is held on the first three days of Shawwal, the tenth month of the Islamic year. This feast, "The Breaking of the Fast," ends the austerities of the month of Ramadan. In 1970 the first day of Shawwal fell on November 30 (A.H. 1390).

IDM. A common kind of gazelle found in the Arabian Peninsula.

IFFAT. A principal wife of His Royal Highness, Faisal, King of Saudi Arabia.

IFRI. A common type of gazelle found in the Arabian Peninsula.

IJMA. In Sunni doctrine, the concept of "universal consent"

as justification for beliefs or practices that are not covered by either the Koran or by the Hadith. The concept of Ijma seems to have grown up rather slowly in the first centuries of Islam and perhaps was an attempt to accommodate the religion to deeply held folk beliefs.

IKHWAN. The Brotherhood of Nejd Bedouins settled by Ibn Saud in agricultural colonies. The first Ikhwan colony was established in the fall of 1912 at the oasis of Artawiya north of Riyadh. Eventually over a hundred of the Ikhwan settlements were formed and these formed a first class group of fighting men for the Saud ruler. As the colonies were religiously oriented (the Ikhwan being fervent Wahhabis) they eventually became somewhat of a problem to the state, especially after the First World War when Saudi Arabia began to deal more and more with foreign powers. In the late 1920's there was increasing unrest and eventually in 1929 an armed uprising against Ibn Saud. Defeated at the battle of Sibila, Ikhwan power quickly declined. At present, by a process of evolution, it has become the Mujahidun or National Guard.

ILB. Arabic name for the tree Ziziphus spina-christi.

IMRUL QAIS. Foremost poet of pre-Islamic times (died ca. 560). He was reared among the Banu Assad and served an apprenticeship as a rawie. See also RAWIE.

IMAM. In Saudi Arabia and other Islamic countries the individual who leads the people in the daily prayers.

INCENSE ROAD. The north-south route over which myrrh and frankincense were transported to the Mediterranean world from Southern Arabia in ancient times. This route ran through the Hejaz and, at least in some periods, touched the cities of Mecca and Medina.

INDIGO. A blue dye formed by the decomposition of indican $(C_{14}H_{17}O_6N)$, a colorless crystalline glucide, into indigotin, a dark blue crystalline compound $(C_{16}H_{10}N_2O_2)$. This dye is produced from the indigo plant (Indigofera tinctoria) which grows in the southwest part of the Arabian Peninsula.

IRON PRODUCTION. Although relatively little iron is pre-

sently mined in Saudi Arabia there are considerable reserves of iron ore in the Kingdom.   In the Wadi Fatima
twenty-five miles east of Jedda are reserves of an estimated forty million tons and some eighty million tons
reserves have been estimated for other areas in the
country.
Iron content of the ore varies somewhat; that in the
Wadi Fatima is forty-five to forty-seven per cent.

IRQ. Long line of sand sometimes reaching the height of
500 to 1000 feet, found in the Rub al Khali.

ISHMAELITES (ISMAILIS).   The Sevener sect of Shia Islam.
See also ISLAM.

ISLAM.   The religion promulgated by Muhammad, now the
faith of 370 to 400 million people.   Islam dates its formal beginnings from the flight or Hegira of the Prophet
Muhammad from Mecca to Yathrib in the Hejaz of western Arabia.   The Hegira took place over a period of
some two months in the year A.D. 622, with the Prophet, and his companion Abu Bakr being the last to
leave.   According to tradition the city of Yathrib was
henceforth called al Medina, "The City" (of the Prophet
Muhammad).
Within ten years of the Hegira, Islam had spread to
much of Arabia, and within a century it had become
(as it remains today) one of the world's great religions.
The basic creed of Islam and the liturgical practices
are relatively simple.   The creed consists of the belief
in one god, in the angels and the prophets, in the revealed writings, and in a day of judgment.   The faith
of Islam rests on four major grounds.   Most important
is the Koran itself, believed by most Moslems to be
an eternal book revealed to Muhammad from an arche-
type in heaven.   The book is collected into 114 suras
or chapters arranged, not chronologically, but in order
of length (the longest first) after a short Sura 1.
To supplement the Koran are a collection of traditions (sunna or "beaten track"), the collection being
referred to as hadith.   In the early Islamic centuries
these collections were codified into six or more standard collections, the most important being the Sahih of
al-Bukhari, which is generally considered canonical.
A third ground on which the faith of Islam rests is
that of qiyas or analogy.   This reasoning developed
slowly over the centuries as more and more moral or

legal situations rose that were not covered by the Koran or by the hadith. The application of analogy, for example, allows devout Moslems to deal with such modern inventions as automobiles, radio and the airplane even though such items were never mentioned in either the Koran or in the hadith.

A fourth and very interesting base for Islamic religion is that of ijma or "consensus." It is based on the tradition that quotes Muhammad saying "my people will never agree in error" and is the vehicle for the absorption of widely held folk beliefs into Islam.

Islam has five obligatory duties:
1. The recitation of the profession of faith
2. Prayer
3. Payment of the zakat or tax of purification on certain kinds of property and on money.
4. Fasting during the month of Ramadan, the ninth month of the Moslem lunar calendar.
5. Pilgrimage (hajj) to Mecca, for each Moslem to perform if at all possible at least once during his lifetime.

During the centuries of its development, Islam has, like all other world religions, seen the growth of sects. Orthodox Islam, today encompassing three-fourths or more of all Moslems, is the Sunni or Sunnite doctrine (i. e., those who have received the sunna, the tradition or customs of Muhammad). In the eighth and ninth centuries four major schools of Sunni Islam grew up, each associated with a major theologian. These are Abu Hanifa of Iraq (died ca. 776) who stressed analogy in his teachings; Ibn Malik of Medina (died ca. 793) who relied heavily on tradition; Ash-Shafi of Egypt (died ca. 820), an eclectic who combined elements of both schools; and Ibn Hanbal of Iraq (died ca. 855) whose Musnad represented the first large collection of hadith. Hanbal was extremely conservative and rejected analogy. The Hanbali school has had recurrent waves of popularity, the most recent being Wahhabism, very influential at present in Saudi Arabia.

The most powerful and influential dissident sect in Islam today is that of Shia, the "Party of Ali." Considering Ali the first legitimate Caliph, the Shias refused to accept the Caliphate in the Umayyad or succeeding Abbasid line. The Shias use the term Imam, "leader," rather than caliph. Shia Islam sees Muhammad as an incarnation of a part of godhead and this "light of Muhammad" was passed on to Ali and then to

Ali's successors. The Imam in Shia Islam probably
has his nearest parallel in the Roman Catholic Pope,
being the fountainhead of religion and having a certain
infallibility. The Shia Imam, however, is also sinless.
Three major Shia sects are called respectively the
"Twelvers" the "Seveners," and the Zeidi. The Twelvers (Ithna Ashariya) believe that (counting from Ali)
there were twelve Imams including both sons of Ali,
Hassan and Hussein. The last Imam was a man
named Muhammad who disappeared around A.D. 875.
The Imamate, however, is supposed to still be in ex-
istence and the Imam, now concealed, will return as
the Mahdi (Guided One) to reform the earth.
Twelver Shia finds its main center in Iran but there
are Twelvers in Iraq and in a number of other countries. The Seveners have similar beliefs but consider
it to have been seventh Imam who disappeared. This
man in Sevener doctrine is Ishmael, while in the
Twelver dogma the seventh Imam was Musa, a younger
brother. The Seveners are sometimes called Ishmaelites or Ismailis. The Fatimids who ruled Egypt in the
eleventh and twelfth century were Ishmaelites, as were
the Hashishin groups (Assassins) and the Druses of
Lebanon. The Khojas of Pakistan who revere the Aga
Khan are also a Sevener offshoot.
The Zeidi, who are very strong in Yemen, claim
descent from Zeid, the grandson of Husein. Zeidis
consider that Zeid's father, Ali Zein al Abidin, the
fourth Imam, forfeited the Imamate by failing to
achieve martyrdom. Zeid was martyred but his family
established a line of succession in Yemen that remains
today.
As Zeid was a student of jurisprudence and was af-
fected by the liberal Mutazilites, later Zeidis followed
the Shafi school and are nearest to Sunni of any Shia
group.
Shia differs from orthodox Islam in having its own
collection of hadith, and in encouraging pilgrimages to
the tombs of Imams, particulary to the tomb of Hussein, the younger son of Ali and Fatima. Shia also
differs in placing greater emphasis on the person of
the Imam. The word Imam used by a Sunni Moslem,
when it refers to historic persons, means one of the
four men who formulated doctrine and law that made up
the four schools of Sunni jurisprudence. Normally,
however, the term is used to refer to the layman who
leads prayers in the mosque.

Other offshoots of Islam include the Bahai faith,
which has become a highly syncratic religion and has
lost any real ties with Shia Islam.   Two modern conservative reformist movements are the Ahmadiyya
movement of India-Pakistan and the Wahhabi of Arabia.
Another movement in Islam that dates from the early
centuries after Muhammad was that of the Sufis and the
Dervish orders, both essentially mystical in nature.
Several other offshoots or variant branches of Islam
have appeared over the centuries.   A number of these
have disappeared.   The group known as Mutazilite
(separatists), who were influential in the eighth to tenth
centuries, attempted to bring a rationalist approach to
religion.   Another early school, the Jabarians or fa-
talists, went to the opposite extreme and defended extreme predestinationism.

The Khawarij or Kharijites who appeared in the first
century of Islam, had a strongly democratic attitude,
holding that any Moslem could theoretically be caliph.
This sect injected itself into the early struggles for
the caliphate when in 661 Kharijites plotted to assassinate both Caliph Ali, son-in-law of the Prophet, and
Muawiya, head of the Umayyad family.   Ali was in
fact killed and his death insured the rise of the Umayyad dynasty.

The Kharijites still exist today in a number of small
sects where they are noted for their strongly literal
interpretation of the Koran.

ITHNA ASHARIYA.   The Twelver sect of Shia Islam.   See
    also ISLAM.

-J-

JABAL (Jebel).   Arabian word for mountain, (pl. Jibil).

JABAL SHAMMAR.   A group of granitic mountains in north-
    ern Saudi Arabia and also the political district in that
    area.   The main town in the Jabal Shammar district
    is Hail, formerly capital of the Rashids.

JAFURA DESERT.   Desert area north of the Rub al Kahli.

JAHILIYA.   The "time of ignorance" of the Koran.   In his-
    toric terms Jahiliya refers to the period of the last
    century or two before Islam and primarily to the areas

of Nejd and Hejaz. In the fifth and sixth centuries A.
D. these were primarily occupied (as they had been for
a very long period) by nomadic Bedouins. A few cities,
primarily Mecca and Yathrib, were beginning to appear
as centers, but the life of the people was primarily
tribal. Because of the absence of contemporary historical sources and because of the relatively little archaeology that has been done in the region, our knowledge
of the Jahiliya is based primarily on secondary literary
sources.

JAUF. A small oasis city near the Persian Gulf and just
      south of the Neutral Zone between Kuwait and Saudi
      Arabia. Jauf was at one time on a major trade route
      from the Persian Gulf via the Wadi Sirhan to the Medi-
      terranean world.

JAZIRAT AL ARAB. The "Island of the Arabs," a common
      name for the Arabian peninsula, so called because of
      the high degree of isolation of the peninsula due to
      desert and inaccessable coastlines.

JEBEL   see JABAL

JEDDA. The chief seaport of Saudi Arabia and the entryway
      for most pilgrims to Mecca, some fifty miles to the
      east. The early history of Jedda is not well known
      but it seems to have been made a port for Mecca in
      A. D. 646 by Caliph Othman. At its present site, how-
      ever, Jedda only dates from the seventeenth century.
          In 1916 the British occupied the city and from the
      end of World War I till 1925 it was ruled by the Hashi-
      mite ruler of Mecca. In that year it was captured by
      Ibn Saud and became part of the Saudi Province of the
      Hejaz.
          In the twentieth century Jedda has been the center
      of foreign legations and embassies, under the Ottoman
      Turks, under the Sherif of Mecca, and, more recently
      under the Saudi kings. In addition, the Saudi Ministry
      of Foreign Affairs is located there.
          The city, at present, has excellent port facilities
      on the Red Sea, and a large airport. The city has
      been largely rebuilt in the last forty years, and a
      modern water system, brought some thirty miles from
      the Wadi Fatima, supplies Jedda with ample water.
      Over 100, 000 pilgrims pass through Jedda each year
      enroute to Mecca or to Medina and hard surfaced roads

lead to each of these cities. The population of Jedda
was estimated in the late 1960's at about 250,000.

JEDDA, DESALINATION PROJECT AT. A large, two stage,
plant for the daily production of some five million gallons of potable water from sea water. This plant,
thought to be the largest in the world, will also produce 50,000 kilowatts of electric power. It was under
construction in 1970.

JEDDA, NATIONAL KING ABDUL AZIZ UNIVERSITY IN.
This private University was opened in 1967-1968 by
King Faisal with a School of Economics and Business
Administration. Plans were made to open three more
faculties: Arts and Humanities, Science and a Girl's
College. In 1970 the University had a faculty of
twenty-four men and fourteen women and a student
body of 265, of which ninety-eight were female.

JEDDA, TREATY OF see TREATY OF JEDDA

JERUSALEM. The third most holy city of Islam (after Mecca and Medina). Jerusalem was overrun by Islamic
armies in A.D. 638 and held by Moslems except for a
century interlude during the Crusades and a few years
of British rule after World War I. The city was occupied by Israeli forces in 1967. It is a focal point
for three major religions: Judaism, Christianity, and
Islam.

JIDD see QIDD

JIDDA see JEDDA

JIHABA. A variety of tuna found in the Persian Gulf and
caught by trolling.

JIHAD. A Holy War against the non-believers or heretics
which, during the Caliphate, was normally proclaimed
by the Caliph and approved by the Ulema.

JIZAN. Coastal city in southern Asir. See also ASIR.

JIZAN, WADI (Asir). Site of one of the largest dams in
Saudi Arabia. The dam is 137 feet high and has a
capacity of some one and a half billion cubic feet of
water.

JUBA. A sandstone depression that extends to the northern border of the Great Nafud. Important oasis towns of the Juba are Jauf and Sakaka.

JUBAIL. A small port city (population ca. 5, 000) on the Persian Gulf between Ras Tanura and Ras al Mishab, which was the first headquarters for technical personnel of ARAMCO.

-K-

KAABA. So named because of its cube-like shape. This structure predated Islam, having a long history in Mecca. It was the shelter of a piece of black meteorite and originally seems to have been made of four walls but without a roof. According to tradition, the Kaaba was destroyed around the beginning of the seventh century and was rebuilt in 608 from timbers of an Abyssinian or Byzantine ship. Around the Kaaba was the sacred precinct common to many Near Eastern cultures. This area, the Haram, was the scene of sacrifices to the gods and also the focus of trading activities.

With the victory of Muhammad the Kaaba was declared to be the sacred center of Islam and the focus for the pilgrims that throughout Islamic history have flocked to Mecca.

KAFFIYEH. A scarf-like head covering worn in Arabia by men. The covering is held in place by the agal and is sometimes called ghutra.

KANAD. Local name for one of the mackerel found in the Persian Gulf and used as a food supply.

KARIA. One of the heliothropes valued as a camel food in eastern Saudi Arabia. Heliotropium digynum.

KAUS. A south wind from the Persian Gulf usually preceding stormy weather.

KEITH, THOMAS. A young Scotsman taken prisoner during the last English expedition against Egypt. As a slave in the service of the Turks, Keith converted to Islam and took the name Ibrahim Aga. He quickly rose in Turkish service and was appointed governor of Medina in 1815. Two months after assuming this post he was

killed by the Wahhabis while traveling to Qasim province.

KHADIJA.   The first wife of the Prophet Muhammad.   A
well-to-do widow of a Meccan merchant, Khadija was
a member of the Quraish and was born around A. D.
555.   She was an employer of the young Muhammad,
sending him on caravan trips.   At the age of about
forty she married the twenty-five year old Muhammad.
Khadija became the first convert to Islam and remained steadfast and faithful to the Prophet and to his
cause till her death around A. D. 619.   While Khadija
lived Muhammad took no other wives.
      Although Khadija bore Muhammad a number of
children, only Fatima, later the wife of Ali, survived
him.

KHAIBAR.   A city in the Northern Hejaz that dates to pre-
Islamic times and has been the object of considerable
archaeological interest in recent years.   Khaibar is on
the main highway which extends from Medina to Tabuk
and beyond.

KHALID BEN AL WALID ("The sword of God").   One of the
leaders of the Meccan party in the early battles between
Muhammad at Medina and his enemies at Mecca.   In
A. D. 625 Khalid commanded the Meccan cavalry and
inflicted a decisive defeat on the Moslem army at Uhud
a few miles from Medina.   In A. D. 627 Khalid was
still commanding cavalry forces against the forces of
Muhammad.
      In A. D. 628 Muhammad returned victoriously to
Mecca and one of his converts was Khalid.   In A. D.
630 Muhammad used this brilliant leader to defeat the
Hawazin and Thakif tribes.
      After Muhammad's death Khalid continued to serve
the Islamic forces as a captain of the first caliph, Abu
Bakr.   In A. D. 633 Khalid crushed the Banu Hanifa
tribe of central Arabia and killed the "false prophet"
Musailima.   In 634, Khalid was again in action, this
time against the Byzantine empire.   In late summer
of that year, Khalid inflicted a sharp defeat on a Byzantine army led by Theodore, brother of the Emperor
Heraclius--this at Ajnadain about twenty miles west of
Jerusalem.   In September 635 Khalid was able to bring
about the capture of Damascus after a six month siege.
His generous treatment of the inhabitants and his pro-

tection of religious liberties and property set a pattern for Islamic conquests for many decades. In the year 636 Heraclius counterattacked with a large army and Khalid temporarily withdrew from Damascus and met the Christian army at the Yarmuk, a small stream that flows into the Jordan River just south of the Sea of Galilee. Here on August 20, 636, the Islamic army overwhelmed the Byzantine forces and within a few months all of Syria was in Moslem hands.

For reasons not now clear Khalid was dismissed by the second caliph Omar shortly after Yarmuk; Khalid had a reputation for cruelty and charges of corruption had been made against him; he may also have seemed a political threat to Omar. There had certainly been considerable displeasure at Khalid for his actions at the battle of Ullais on the Persian Gulf in 633. At that battle Khalid and the Bedouin Muthanna of the Bakr tribe allowed a mass killing of Persian and Christian prisoners. From Ullais the two pushed on to Hira on the Syrian front and Muthanna was attacked by the Persian general, Rustam. Near the site of ancient Babylon, Rustam caught the Islamic forces trying to cross the Euphrates and destroyed the Arab army, Mutanna being killed.

KHALID, TRIBE OF. The Banu Khalid are an important tribe in the Hasa that were incorporated into the first Saudi state in the year 1790.

KHAMIS MUSHAIT. A small city in Asir in the highlands some fifty miles northeast of the highland district capital of Abha. Khamis Mushait is best known for its Himyarite inscriptions. See also ARABIA, HISTORY OF--EARLY PERIOD.

KHARJ. An important agricultural district some sixty miles south of Riyadh. The Kharj is well watered due to its position east of the Tuwaiq escarpment. In 1970 the Saudi Ministry of Agriculture had set aside 87,029 acres of land in Al Kharj for agricultural settlement and much of this land has been distributed.

There are important archaeological resources in Kharj including remnants of irrigation systems.

KHASH. An Arabic word for nose, which can also mean an escarpment or a promontory.

KHOBAR. A trading town and surrounding district of some
35,000 population. Khobar is situated only a few miles
east of Dhahran, which is a major trade outlet for
Khobar.

KHOBAR DESALINATION PROJECT. A large sea water desalination project that will produce some seven and a
half million gallons of water per day. This plant is
expected to cost about fifteen million dollars.

KHURMA. Town in western central Saudi Arabia some 100
miles west of Taif on the Wadi Safui. Khurma lies
south of the main highway from Taif to Riyadh but has
recently been connected to it by an all weather road.
    The town has considerable historical importance in
Saudi Arabian history. Located on the Nejd-Hejaz
border, it opted for Saudi rule but, because of British
political machinations during World War I, was given
to Hussein of the Hejaz. Saudi Arabia was ordered by
the British to relinquish the region on pain of losing a
current British subsidy of Ł 60,000 per year.
    In May 1919, with British approval, an army under
Abdulla, second son of Hussein, marched to occupy
Khurma. His army was intercepted by Saudi forces
at Turaba, eighty miles west of Khurma and largely
wiped out.

KHUTBAH. The sermon preached in a mosque at Friday
noon and on certain special occasions.

KIYAS see QIYAS

KORAN (Al Quran, The Book or the Reading). Sacred scripture of the Islamic world. The Koran consists of the
utterances of the Prophet Muhammad (c. A.D. 570-632).
To Moslems, the Koran is divine revelation.
    The Koran was begun very early in Muhammad's
ministry, certainly in the first Meccan period. Later
tradition holds that the initial revelation came at a hill
named Hira near Mecca. In the month of Ramadan,
probably around A.D. 610 Muhammad, while in a
trance, heard the Angel Gabriel recite words that now
form part of Sura 96. Three times a voice charged
the Prophet to "read." After the third repetition of
this command, Muhammad asked "What can I read?"
and the voice recited the sura which begins.
    Read: in the name of thy Lord who createth
    Who createth man from a clot

Muhammad at first told only a few people, members
of his family and close friends, of the message, but
after three years, a revelation that was to form Sura
74 called on him to rise. From that time Muhammad
began openly to preach to the people of Mecca.
As the religion spread so did the opposition and in
A. D. 622 (the Hegira) Muhammad was forced to flee
to the city of Yathrib or Medina.
At Medina there continued to be revelations and on
the victorious return of Muhammad to Mecca there
followed still others.   Ten years after the Hegira, in
the year A. D. 632, the Prophet died.
Even before Muhammad's death some, perhaps most,
of the Koran had been written down, but until his death,
new chapters (suras) were constantly being added and
the holy book was probably mainly recited orally.
It soon became clear in the years following the
Prophet's death that a canonical version of the Koran
was needed for separate versions soon sprang up.   Under the caliphate of Othman (644-656) an authorized
version was made.

KORAN, ABROGATED VERSES.   A strange and not completely understood affair in the pre-Medina days of Islam.   At some time around A. D. 615, Muhammad announced that he had received a revelation legitimizing
the worship of three popular goddesses of Mecca,
Manat, al Lat, and al Uzza.   The words of Sura 53,
verse 19, are: "Al-Lat, al-Uzza, and Manat are the
exalted virgins whose intercession may be counted on."
As a main thrust of the new religion was to deny
the reality of pagan deities this announcement led to
confusion among adherents of the new faith.   A short
time after the "revelations" Muhammad announced that
Satan himself had tricked him into uttering falsehoods,
and the verses were withdrawn.   The canonical reading
of Sura 53, especially verse 20, is uncompromisingly
monotheistic and of the goddesses it is said, "They
are but names which you have named, you and your
fathers, for which Allah has revealed no warrant."
It is not possible at this late date to be sure what
really happened.   Perhaps the Prophet intended to
make some small concession in a last effort to concili-
ate his enemies among the Meccans, an attempt that--
in any case--was surely doomed to failure.   In the absence of a clear historical picture of the times it is
probably best to accept the traditional version of the
event.

KUWAIT, AMIRATE OF. A small principality in the north-
    east corner of Arabia, also the name of the principal
    city. Kuwait has had in the late nineteenth and early
    twentieth centuries very important relationships with
    the Saudi rulers. The large scale production of oil in
    Kuwait in the 1950's made the Amirate one of the
    richest small states in the world--the production of
    crude oil in 1969, for example, was over one billion
    barrels. Kuwait and Saudi Arabia share an oil rich
    area officially called the Neutral Zone. Population of
    Kuwait in 1970 is given at 733,196 and the area is
    7450 square miles.

-L-

LABOR RELATIONS. Labor legislation is very new in Saudi
    Arabia, the first such law being the Labor and Work-
    men Regulation promulgated in 1946. This regulation,
    as modified in 1951, prohibits child labor and sets up
    a forty-eight hour week with pay for days off and for
    official holidays. The regulation also contains detailed
    rules concerning working conditions, sick and disability
    indemnity and arbitration procedures. These regula-
    tions were considerably revised and updated in the late
    1960's. Labor matters in general are handled by the
    Saudi Ministry of Labor and Social Affairs.

LAND USE   see AGRICULTURE AND LAND USE

LANGUAGES   see ARABIA, HISTORY OF--EARLY PERIOD;
    ARABIC SCRIPT

LAWRENCE OF ARABIA   see LAWRENCE, THOMAS ED-
    WARD

LAWRENCE, THOMAS EDWARD (1888-1935). British ex-
    plorer and statesman. Lawrence was born in Wales
    on August 15, 1888, the second of five brothers. He
    studied at Oxford taking a first in modern history in
    1910. That same year Lawrence made a trip through
    Syria and began to apply himself to learning spoken
    Arabic. He became a friend of David George Hogarth,
    who combined a position in archaeology at the Ashmo-
    lean museum with activity in British Intelligence.
        Under Hogarth's direction, Lawrence excavated at
    Carchemish from 1911 to 1914, at which time he also

spent a considerable amount of time traveling in Syria
and Mesopotamia.

With the beginning of World War I, Lawrence was
sent by Lord Kitchener to Egypt where he helped to form
a Military Intelligence Service. Eventually Lawrence
was shifted to Jedda where, under the British Arab
Service, he was a major architect in British policy
that backed the Sherif Hussein of Mecca. Working with
Emir Faisal, the son of Hussein, and with a brother of
Faisal, Abdulla, Lawrence raided behind the Turkish
lines as far north as Syria. He was a prime mover in
the disabling of the Damascus to Medina Railroad.

In the post war period, Lawrence struggled at the
Paris Peace Conference to fulfill some of his wartime
promises to the Arabs, especially to the House of Hussein. He soon found that Syria, which he had hoped to
make independent, was to be turned over to the French.
Disgusted by what he considered the duplicity of the
British government, Lawrence retired from politics.
He enlisted in the British Royal Air Force in 1922 as
a mechanic. The following year Lawrence joined the
tank corps but rejoined the RAF in 1925, serving for
a time in India. Lawrence returned to England in
1928 and resigned from military service in March 1935.
A few weeks later he was killed in a motorcycle acci-
dent.

LEILA (Ghusiba). Population ca. 5000, the principal town in
the Aflaj province. The old city of Leila is located
on a small oasis less than a square mile in extent.

LENAHAN, W. J. Representative of the Standard Oil Company of California when oil was found in the Hasa in
commercial quantities in 1938.

LOZ. Peak in the Aqaba region reaching 8, 461 feet.

-M-

MADAIN SALIH. A small city in the northern Hejaz, the
site of an extensive archaeological area, with elabo-
rately decorated buildings carved from solid rock.

MADANI, AL see ABDULLA IBN IBRAHIM AL NAJDI

MAGHAZI. The history of the campaigns of the Prophet

Muhammad compiled by the scholar Al Waqidi (died A.
D. 822).

MAHAD DHAHAB.   Gold mining area some 100 miles southeast of Medina and also name of a nearby town in the
Hejaz province.   The goldmining here is ancient (the
name means "cradle of gold").   Two major areas of
tailings have been found, the newest representing work-
ings of ca. A. D. 750-1000 and the oldest perhaps a
thousand years earlier.   These still contain a considerable amount of gold.
    The Mahad Dhahab mines have been worked by the
Saudi Arabian Mining Syndicate Ltd., but mining policy
is at present being restudied by the Saudi Arabian government.

MAHMAL.   The Nejdi district of the middle Hanifa drainage
just north of Riyadh.

MAJIDI.   A Turkish silver coin used for a time in Saudi
Arabia.   Foreign coinage in Saudi Arabia has now been
superceded by the riyal system of coinage.

MALIKI.   One of the four schools of jurisprudence that appeared in orthodox (Sunni) Islam in the eighth and ninth
centuries A. D.   The Malikis believed that great im-
portance should be placed on the body of traditions,
the hadith, in supplementing and rounding out the Koran.   For example, when a situation arises that is not
covered by specific statements in the Koran, the Maliki
position was that the hadith should be consulted, and if
no precedent could be found the situation should be re-
solved by the theological scholars of Medina.
    The Maliki school was named for its founder, Ibn
Malik of Medina, who died around A. D. 793.

MANAMA.   City on Bahrein Island and capital of Bahrein.

MANASIR.   One of the very large tribal groupings of the
Near Eastern deserts.   There are six separate Manasir tribes, three living in Iraq, one living in Jordan,
one in Asir, and the sixth in the Trucial states and
in Eastern Saudi Arabia.

MANAT ("Fate").   The goddess whose sanctuary was at
Wudayd on the highroad between Mecca and Yathrib
(Medina).   Manat was one of the goddesses involved in

the abrogated verses of the Koran. Manat was especially favored by the two major tribes of Yathrib, the Khazraj and the Aws.

MARIB. Sabaean city some hundred miles northeast of Sana in Yemen.

MARIB, DAM OF. A large dam and irrigation project built in Sabaean times and producing a large fertile area around Marib some hundred miles northeast of Sana.

MASALEEKH. Subdivision of the large Anaza tribe to which the Saudi family belongs.

MECCA. The most holy city of all Islam and the center of annual pilgrimages from all over the Islamic world. Situated in the central Hejaz, Mecca is below the escarpment that provides Mecca's sister town and agricultural supplier, Taif, with a pleasant climate. In Mecca temperatures often become ovenlike and the area is rather barren.
   Mecca was well established in pre-Islamic times. It was known to the geographer Ptolemy as Macoraba, and by the sixth century A.D. was an important center on the spice road from southern Arabia to the Mediterranean world and was perhaps the most important cult center in northern Arabia. In Muhammad's time the tribe of the Quraish dominated the life of the city; Muhammad himself was a member of the Hashimite clan of this tribe. Although the Prophet of Islam left Mecca for Medina in A.D. 622 and, indeed, is buried at that city, Mecca was designated the primate city of Islam and the central area of the city, the Haram, with the legendary well of Zamzam and the Kaaba, became and remains the major pilgrimage point of Moslems all over the world.
   Throughout the history of Islam, Mecca was usually under the control of one or another outside power, but in the period of the Ottoman Empire it maintained a considerable measure of autonomy under the rule of the Qitada family, Hashimite rulers or sherifs of the city. Mecca was twice part of the Saudi Empire, once from 1803 to 1813 (though the city was disputed with the local Qitada ruler) and again when the forces of King Ibn Saud entered the city in October 13, 1924.
   Since the incorporation of Mecca into Saudi Arabia, the city has been generally enhanced by a building pro-

gram that began in 1955, following the completion of
reconstruction of the Prophet's Mosque at Medina.
The region around the Kaaba, the Holy Mosque area,
was greatly enlarged, allowing some 300,000 pilgrims
to pray together, all with a good view of the sacred
structure.
        At Mecca are situated the Saudi College of Educa-
tion and the Sharia and Islamic Studies College.   The
city is on a major highway that runs from Jedda to
Riyadh.   Present population is estimated at 200,000.

MECCA, HOLY MOSQUE OF.   The Mosque of the Kaaba in
        the pilgrimage city of Mecca.   This mosque was much
        enlarged in the period after 1955.

MECCA, SHERIFS OF   see SHERIFS OF MECCA

MEDICINE   see HEALTH SERVICES AND MEDICINE

MEDINA.   The second (after Mecca) most holy city of Islam.
        Medina is located in the northern Hejaz, some 200
        miles northeast of Mecca in a large oasis.   It is sur-
        rounded by six valleys, the best known being the Wadi
        al Aqiq.   Originally titled Yathrib, the city was pros-
        perous at least by the sixth century A.D., being on
        one of the main spice routes from the area of southern
        Arabia to the Syrian and Palestinean areas.   According
        to traditional accounts the city was originally settled
        by members of the Banu Qaila, a tribe from what is
        present-day Yemen.   At the time of Muhammad it was
        controlled by two main pagan tribes, the Aws and the
        Khazraj, plus a number of Jewish groups, probably
        Judaized Arabians or Aramaeans.   In Islam tradition,
        the name Yathrib was changed to Medina (Arab. for
        "The City" [of the Prophet]), after Muhammad's arri-
        val in A.D. 622; however, the name may have been
        introduced by Aramaic speaking Jews and may have
        been originally the Aramaic word "Medinta."
        Medina became the center of early Islamic political
        power and Muhammad, himself, lies buried there.
        The first three Caliphs ruled from Medina but follow-
        ing the rise of the Omayyad Dynasty political power
        passed from Arabia.
        At present the city of Medina is an important agri-
        cultural center, being noted for date groves.   It was
        the southern terminus of the old Damascus-Medina
        railroad destroyed in World War I.   Today, Medina is

connected by modern road southward to Jedda and Mecca south northward to Tabuk, and eastward to Riyadh. A road northeastward to Hail is presently planned. The city is famous for its historic spots, the best known being the Mosque of the Prophet where Muhammad lies buried. This structure was begun in A.D. 622 and is the prototype of all mosques. In 1946 King Ibn Saud announced his plan to enlarge this mosque and this project was completed under King Saud in 1955.

Medina is the site of the famous Islamic University with students from more than sixty countries. At present it has a television station, and several new hotels. The population of Medina is approximately 100,000.

MEDINA, ISLAMIC UNIVERSITY OF. This University is the major Saudi institution for instruction in the Sharia. It has a present budget of more than two million dollars annually. The University is located on the west bank of the Wadi al Aqiq and has three faculties; Sharia, Islamic Call, and Principles of Religion. Nearly a thousand students from all parts of the world are currently enrolled in this University; for example, in 1967, sixty-three nations from Asia, Africa, Europe, and the Americas were represented.

MEDINA, PROPHETS MOSQUE. Mosque of the tomb of the Prophet Muhammad. This mosque was restored and enlarged in the period 1951-1955.

MESA. Mesa is a Spanish word meaning table, but also refers to flat hills or rock outcroppings that rise above the surrounding landscape. The word mesa is widely used in this latter sense in desert and semi-desert areas and often occurs in the literature of Arabia.

MIDIAN. District of Saudi Arabia that borders the Gulf of Aqaba and the extreme northeast portion of the Red Sea.

MINA. A village a few miles from the city of Mecca where pilgrims stay the night before the ceremony at the Plain of Arafat. See ARAFAT, STANDING ON.

MINAEAN. During the first millenium B.C., one of the earliest states in southwestern Arabia. See also ARABIA, HISTORY OF--EARLY PERIOD.

MINERALS AND MINING. A number of commercially valuable minerals have been found in Saudi Arabia. These include barite, flourite, magnesite, salt, sulphur, silica, clay, chromium, feldspar, asbestos, gypsum, and limestone, granite, slate, and marble. Exploitation of these minerals and the various metals are under the control of the Saudi Arabian Ministry of Petroleum and Mineral Resources. Though there is as yet relatively little commercial exploitation of minerals, gypsum production for the Kingdom reached 25, 705 tons in 1969 and cement production that same year was put at 5 75, 636 tons. (See also under individual metals, e. g., GOLD, SILVER).

MITAB IBN ABDULLA. Brother of the Rashid ruler Talil, Mitab ruled from 1866 to 1868 in Hail.

MOOSE, JAMES S. , JR. American diplomat who opened a legation in Jedda in 1942. Until that time United States-Saudi Arabia affairs were handled by the American minister in Cairo.

MOSES. The lawgiver of Christian and Judaic tradition. Moses is also a revered by Moslems.

MOSLEM. An adherent to Islam. Sometimes spelled Muslim.

MOSQUE. From the Arabic masjid derived from sajada "to bend or to adore (or to pray)." The Moslem place of worship. The first mosque was built in Medina during the lifetime of the Prophet Muhammad. It was a crude building of mud brick with a roof of palm branches supported with palm trunks. In this mosque the faithful prayed facing Jerusalem. After the death of Muhammad and the spread of Islam, more ambitious mosques were built. Outside of Arabia, mosques were built very early at Jerusalem, Fustat (the Predecessor to modern Cairo) and Kufa (in the lower Euphrates valley). As the Arabs quickly met and conquered peoples who were skilled in architecture, the mosque became more elaborate until it was a major triumph of Arabian architecture.
    Early features of mosques that appeared in the first century after the death of Muhammad include the Mihrab, a praying niche in which the faithful could face Mecca to pray. The mihrab was in use in Da-

mascus by the time of the first Syrian caliph, Muawiya
(that is by A.D. 660).   This feature was not universal;
in Egypt originally a stone was set up to point the direction to Mecca and in Mesopotamia in the eighth century mosques were built with three arched openings
that substituted for the mihrab.   Another feature of
mosques that appeared very early was the raised plat-
form, or pulpit, which appeared in Egypt and probably
was copied from the similar structure in the Christian
church.   Still another, the minaret (the word derives
from the Manara or lighthouse tower of Alexandria)
took the place of the Christian bell tower.   Other features of the mosque include the courtyard with a font
for ritual cleansing, and the dome, the latter contri-
buted by newly Moslemized Mediterranean peoples.

Famous early mosques include the Dome of the Rock
in Jerusalem, and the Great Mosque at Damascus.

Unlike Christianity, the Islamic mosque has no elaborate group of priestly functionaries attached.   The
five daily prayers (at dawn, midday, midafternoon, sunset, evening) may be led by any Moslem of good standing though they usually are led by an imam, a pious
man who devotes part of his time to these religious
duties.   Worshippers remove their shoes and after certain ritual abolutions they form a line facing Mecca
and repeat a series of prayers beginning with the
words "God is greater than all" and ending with "Peace
be with you and the mercy of God."

Mosques are also places of private prayer and medi-
tation and are used for this purpose by both sexes.

MUFTI.   A man authorized to teach and expound on the Is-
     lamic religious code, particularly that as given in the
     Hanbali teachings.   The Grand Mufti of Saudi Arabia
     is the head of the Ulema.

MUHAMMAD (The Prophet of Islam) (ca. A.D. 570-630).
     Founder of the religion of Islam.   Born into the Hashi-
     mite clan of the tribe of Quraish at Mecca, Muhammad
     removed to Medina in A.D. 622 (the Hegira) and the
     first great successes of Islam were directed from that
     city.   Because the life and teachings of Muhammad are
     major facts of both Arabic and Islamic history, further
     information on the Prophet will be found under ARABIA,
     HISTORY OF--ISLAMIC PERIOD.

MUHAMMAD ALI.   Pasha or ruler of Egypt under the Otto-

man Turks who, in the period 1814-1818 broke up the
first Saudi Empire, capturing the Saudi capital of Dariya in the Wadi Hanifa in 1818.   See also DARIYA;
SAUDI ARABIA, HISTORY OF.

MUHAMMAD AL IDRISI.   Ruler of Asir during the first
World War period.   Recognized as the legitimate head
of that country by the English because of his anti-
Turkish activities, Muhammad was quickly challenged
by the Aidh brothers, Hassan and Muhammad, who as
chieftains of Abha had been faithful to the Turks.   The
Aidhs brought in Saudi help.   The Wahhabi forces were
eager to comply, opposing the Idrisi on religious
grounds and in 1920-1926 absorbed Asir into the Saudi
Kingdom.

MUHAMMAD IBN ABDULLA IBN RASHID.   Most successful
of the Rashidi of Hail, ruled from 1872 to 1897.   During Muhammad's reign the Rashids overran much of
Nejd including the Saudi capital of Riyadh.

MUHAMMAD IBN ABDUL WAHHAB (1703-1792).   The religious reformer whose teachings are the basis of Saudi
Arabian religious and political thought.   Muhammad
was born in the town of Ayaina in the central Wadi
Hanifa area.   Muhammad's father was Qadi or religious
judge in Ayaina and belonged to the Hanbali school of
Islamic jurisprudence.   Muhammad was a precocious
scholar, memorizing the Koran by the age of ten, according to one tradition.   A few years later Muhammad traveled to Hejaz and studied for a time at Medina.   Returning to Ayaina he began to put into effect
the puritanical form of Islam as taught by Hanbal and
by a later Hanbali scholar, Taimiya of Damascus.
Muhammad Abdul Wahhab was especially disturbed at
the violations of the Koran and the Hadith that occurred
all over Arabia and the tendency to icon worship and
idolatry common in his day.   Muhammad and his followers called themselves Muwahhidun (Unitarians) and
this is the official name of the movement, though the
name Wahhabism is commonly used today.
    An early attempt to preach Wahhabism at Basra in
Iraq failed and Muhammad then launched the movement
in his home town.   Eventually he was forced to flee to
Dariya where, around 1740 a covenant was made with
Amir Muhammad ibn Saud in which Wahhabism was to
be the religion of the rising Saudi State.   Under Mu-

hammad ibn Saud and his son, Abdul Aziz ibn Muhammad, Wahhabism flourished; Muhammad ibn Abdul Wahhab remaining in Dariya as a powerful counselor and advisor until his death.

Wahhabism is an extremely literal interpretation of Islam, drawing on the Koran and the Hadith and rejecting Qiyas or analogy. The Wahhabis discourage relics of all kinds and special sacred buildings, especially tombs. Alcohol and tobacco are forbidden, as is most music. The lax behavior of people of the Hejaz was long a source of Wahhabi irritation and since the Saudi conquest of the Hejaz strict reforms have been made in that area. King Ibn Saud, however, restrained the reformers from interfering with pilgrims.

MUHAMMAD IBN SAUD (1735-1766). Amir of Dariya, the Saudi ruler that became a convert of the puritanical reformer Muhammad ibn Abdul Wahhab. Muhammad Ibn Saud instituted the outlines of the political and religious pact that has guided Saudi fortunes to the present day.

MUHAMMAD, WIVES OF. Although sources differ, the following probably represents a reasonably comprehensive list of the women married to the Prophet.

Khadija bint Khuwaylid--of the Quraish tribe in Mecca. Khadija was Muhammad's first and only wife till her death. She was about forty years of age at the time of the marriage, ca. A. D. 595.

Sawda bint Zama of the Quraish tribe whom Muhammad married about 620 when she was some thirty years old.

Aisha bint Abu Bakr of the Quraish tribe, the only virgin married by Muhammad, in 623, when she was nine years old.

Hafsa bint Omar of the Quraish tribe, married in A. D. 625, aged about eighteen.

Umm Salama bint al Mughira of the Quraish tribe, married in 626 at the age of twenty-nine.

Zaynab bint Khuzayma married in 625 or 626, aged about thirty.

Juwayriya, married in 627, aged twenty.

Zaynab bint Jahsh, married in 627, aged thirty-eight.

Mariya the Copt, 628 or earlier; Mariya however, remained a concubine.

Umm Habiba bint Abi Sufyan of the Quraish, married in 628, aged about thirty-five.

Shafiya bint Huyayy, a Jewish woman captured at Khaybar in 628, aged seventeen. Originally a concubine, she embraced Islam and was freed.

Maymuna bint al Harith, married in A.D. 629, aged twenty-seven.

Rayhana bint Zayd, another Jewish woman captured with the Bani Quraish in 627 and became a concubine of Muhammad. She was never freed and died in 632.

This group of thirteen--eleven wives and two important concubines, one who bore Muhammad a son, are reasonably authenticated. Of the group three died before Muhammad.

A number of other women have been associated with the Prophet but the situation is not clear enough to be sure that any one of them formed a lasting union with Muhammad.

MUJAHIDUN. The National Guard of present day Sauda Arabia. See also IKHWAN.

MURRA, AL. One of the large tribes of east central Arabia. The Murra center on the northeastern part of the Rub al Khali, ranging as far west as the Jafura district west of Qatar and south of Hofuf. One eastern center of the Murra is Jabrin, an oasis some 150 miles south of Hofuf, where several hundred families live by combining date farming with herding. It was to Jabrin that Abdul Rahman, ruler of the house of Saud, fled when Riyadh was captured by the ruler of Hail, Muhammad ibn Rashid in 1891. From Jabrin the Saud family moved to Kuwait and then launched the successful reoccupation of Riyadh. In the early struggles between the reviving Saudi forces and the House of Rashid, the Murra tribe maintained loyalty to the Saudi side.

MURZOUQ. Khuwiya or bodyguard to King Faisal of Saudi Arabia. Murzouq and Faisal were boys together and Murzouq was in attendance on the king in a number of his foreign travels, including the wartime trip to the United States.

MUSALMAN. In Persian an adherent to Islam, or Moslem.

MUSCAT AND OMAN. Oman is an independent state in the southwestern corner of the Arabian Peninsula. It has an area of ca. 82,000 square miles, and a population

of about 550,000 to 600,000.   The most important city
is Muscat.   Although the population of Oman is pre-
dominately Arab-speaking and the principle religion is
Islam, Oman also has cultural ties with India.
   The present state is of recent vintage.   The Sul-
tanate of Muscat and Oman in the nineteenth century
was to a considerable degree, under British control.
In 1913 a serious tribal rebellion created a virtually
autonomous state in the interior of the country, (the
Imamate of Oman), a situation which was recognized
by the 1920 Treaty of Sib.   More recently in the period
around 1960 the Sultan of Muscat and Oman, with British
help, reestablished effective control over most of the
country.   The situation has been complicated by the discovery of large oil reserves in 1963.

MUTAWWA.   A Wahhabi missionary.   Such missionaries were
   used by Ibn Saud to spread Wahhabi reforms and Saudi
   rule.

MUTHANNA.   A leader of the Bakr tribe of the Bahrein area.
   In A.D. 633 Muthanna and the great Muslim leader,
   Khalid ben al Walid, defeated a mixed army of Persians and Christian Arabs at Ullais.   This victory was
   marred by a mass killing of prisoners, which action
   may have been a factor in the later dismissal of Khalid
   by Omar, the second Caliph.   At any rate Muthanna
   and Khalid pushed on northward and captured Hira and
   Anbar on the lower Euphrates River.   The Arabs were
   now in a position to threaten Ctesiphon, the Sassanid
   Persian capital, on the Tigris and perhaps capture the
   boy king Yazdegerd.   Khalid, however, was called away
   to the Syrian front and Muthanna was left with much
   depleted forces.   In November, 634 the Persian general Rustam attacked Muthanna's forces, who were at-
   tempting to cross the Euphrates near the ruins of
   Babylon.   The Persian elephants caused the Arab cavalry horses to bolt and the Arabs were crushingly defeated at this Battle of the Bridge.   Muthanna was ser-
   iously wounded and soon died as a result of these
   wounds.

MUWAHHIDUN (Unitarians).   The term Muhammad ibn Abdul
   Wahhab and his followers used to designate their reform
   movement within the Hanbali school of Sunni jurisprudence.   The term Wahhabi is now more commonly used.
   See also MUHAMMAD IBN ABDUL WAHHAB.

MUZZEIN.   In Islamic countries the individual who issues
the call to prayer.

MYRRH.   The resin from a low spreading cedar-like tree
with a central trunk, Balsamodendron myrrha.   The
resin is collected by cutting and peeling the bark of
the tree in short strips.   This operation, done in the
summer, allows globules of resin to collect and to
harden.   These are collected in the fall.   Myrrh was
traded to the Mediterranean world at least as early as
the Egyptian Old Kingdom (mid-third millenium B. C.)
and was used primarily as an ingredient in cosmetics
and perfumes.   Like frankincense, which is grown in
much the same areas, myrrh comes from the mountain
areas of Yemen and the Hadramaut, and is also found
in Somalia.
    Myrrh is red-brown in color; a rare white variety
is produced in Abyan north and east of Aden.
    The resin is still an important trade item in Arabia,
as is that of frankincense.

-N-

NAFUD.   Anglicized Arabic word for sand desert.   The
Great Nafud in northern Saudi Arabia is an example.
In southern Arabia, the term Ramla tends to be used
instead of Nafud.

NAFUD DAHI.   Desert area in western Nejd west of the Tuwaiq Escarpment extending from the Wadi Dawasir in
the south to the Wadi Sirra in the north.

NAFUD, GREAT   see GREAT NAFUD

NAIM TRIBE.   Tribal group in the Buraimi Oasis, an area
long disputed between Saudi Arabia and Britain.   In the
eighteenth century the Naim were the dominant power
in the area; though from 1800 to about 1870 they were
subject to Nejd.   The Naim occupy the villages of
Buraimi proper, Saara, and Hamasa.

NAJD   see NEJD

NAJRAN.   A series of oases on the eastern flank of the
mountains of Asir, also the chief town of the region.
As part of the general settlement following the Saudi-

Yemen war of 1933-1934, Najran was incorporated into
the kingdom of Saudi Arabia, though administered sepa-
rately from Asir.   At present Najran is part of an ambitious plan for agricultural development, some 100,000
acres being set aside for agricultural reclamation in
the area.

NEFUD   see NAFUD

NEGROES   see RACES IN SAUDI ARABIA

NEJD.   The uplands of northeast central Arabia.   Although
without absolute fixed boundaries, the Nejd is bounded
on the west by the Hejaz range and on the east by the
Dahna, a tongue of sand that connects Arabia's two
main sandy deserts, the Great Nafud on the north and
the Rub al Khali on the south and east.   These deserts
in turn form the northern and southern (or more accu-
rately, the northwestern and southeastern) boundaries
of the Nejd.   The province basically slopes from the
west and south to the east and north, the slope being
broken by a series of west-facing granitic mountains
whose eastern slopes continue the gentle decline toward
the east and north.   The Dahna has an average width
of some thirty miles and is four hundred miles long,
being characterized in its northern portion by peaks
of red sand sometimes several hundred feet high.
     There are three main stream systems in the Nejd,
all of them intermittent, and all draining generally
from west to east.   The Wadi al Rumma rises not far
from Khaibar, north of Medina, and flows eastward to
the Dahna where it disappears, resuming its course
east of the desert under the name Wadi al Batin.   It
then continues to a point near Zubair in Iraq, near the
Tigris-Euphrates mouth, some 600 miles from its
source.   The Wadi al Surra rises in western Nejd and
flows eastward joing the Wadi Hanifa at Yamama forty
miles south and east of Riyadh.   From this area under
the new name Wadi al Sahba, the river course continues to the Persian Gulf near Qatar.   A third wadi
is the Dawasir which has its source near Bisha in the
Asir mountains and flows eastward to disappear in the
Rub al Khali.
     The Nejd is extremely hot in summer, but the ef-
fect of the heat is somewhat lessened by the great dry-
ness of the area.   Winters tend to be cool; a February temperature as low as 18° F. has been reported

from Hail in the Jabal Shammar of northern Nejd.
Rainfall seldom exceeds five inches per year, falling
mostly in the winter months. The northern Nejd receives some effects from rain bearing west winds
blowing off the Mediterranean. Elsewhere south winds
from the Arabian Sea blowing across the faces of the
mountains produces the small amount of rain.
Population centers important in the history of Arabia and in her contemporary life include Hail in the
north, the center of the Rashid dynasty that controlled
much of the Nejd in the latter part of the nineteenth
century. Farther south and east, in the Wadi Hanifa
is the old Saudi Capital of Dariya and a few miles to
the south and east, the present capital of Riyadh.
From a view point of recent history the Nejd is famous as the home of the early Saudi rulers who had
settled in Dariya as rulers in the fifteenth century.
The Nejd was also the home of Muhammad ibn Wahhab
who was born at Uyaina in the upper Wadi Hanifa and
who by his alliance with the house of Saud moulded
and directed the later history of Arabia.

NEUTRAL ZONES. Two disputed areas, one between Saudi
Arabia and Iraq, just west of Kuwait and the other between Saudi Arabia and Kuwait to the south of Kuwait.
The Neutral Zone between the Saudi Kingdom and Kuwait is more important. It is 2, 200 square miles and
has extensive oil deposits which are extracted jointly
by Saudi Arabia and Kuwait. In 1969 oil production in
this Neutral Zone was approximately 145 million barrels divided equally between Kuwait and Saudi Arabia.
The second Neutral Zone, that between Saudi Arabia
and Iraq is larger (7, 000 square miles) but is, at present, of relatively little economic value.

NEWSPAPERS IN SAUDI ARABIA. Organized under the Min-
istry of Information there are at present a number of
both daily and weekly newspapers in the kingdom.
There is no official censorship of the press. Daily
newspapers include (as of 1969):
Mecca. Al Nadwa, founded in 1963, distribution
10, 000 copies.
Dammam. Al Yaum, 1964, dist. 4, 500.
Jedda. Medina Al Munawwarah, 1955, dist. 9, 500.
Jedda. Okadh, 1964, dist. 11, 000.
Jedda. Al Belad, 1963, dist. 8, 900.
Riyadh. Al Riyadh, 1965, dist. 8, 900.
Riyadh. Riyadh Daily Newsletter, 1967, dist. 400.

NIEBUHR, KARSTEN (1733-1815). Danish explorer, Member and only survivor of the 1761 Danish expedition to Arabia. Born in Germany Niebuhr received little formal education, but taught himself surveying and geography, and also learned some Arabic. Niebuhr's survival of the expedition is attributed to the fact that he adopted native dress and ate native food. Although untrained, he was a careful observer and his works on Arabia are classics. Niebuhr married in 1773 and was in the Danish military service for some time following his Arabia trip. When he died in 1815 he held a position in the civil service of Holstein.

NORTHERN FRONTIERS PROVINCE. The large administrative area of Saudi Arabia lying north of Nejd and including the eastern border with Jordan (the Wadi Sirhan region) and the western part of the Saudi-Iraqi border as far as the Neutral Zone between those two countries.

-O-

OASIS (Plural, Oases). From Coptic words meaning to dwell and to drink. Oases are desert areas that, because of the availability of water, are fertile. In the Arabian Peninsula underground water may drain for hundreds of miles from the western highlands to the lower eastern areas and then surface in springs or wells. There are numbers of oases in the Hanifa, in the Hasa at Kharj, and a number of other areas. See also WATER RESOURCES AND DEVELOPMENT.

OIL PRODUCTION, SAUDI ARABIA. The Eastern Province of Saudi Arabia and the Neutral Zone between Saudi Arabia and Kuwait accounted in 1969 for some 1,173 million American barrels (one American barrel equalling 135.13 kgs.) of crude oil, thus making Saudi Arabia the fifth largest producer in the world. Of this vast quantity of crude oil, ARAMCO wells produced 93%, the Japanese owned Arabian Oil Company, Ltd., operating in the Neutral Zone off shore produced 5% and Getty Oil Company cooperating with the Kuwait based Aminoil Company produced 2%.

Though most of the Saudi Arabian oil is exported, distribution of both oil and refined petroleum products within Arabia is done through Petromin, a Saudi state

corporation. In 1969 the kingdom of Saudi Arabia had
an oil consumption of 12, 872, 228 barrels.

OMAN   see MUSCAT AND OMAN

-P-

PALGRAVE, WILLIAM GIFFORD (1826-1888). A British
infantry officer in Bombay who converted to Roman
Catholicism in the 1840's, was ordained a priest and
joined the Jesuit order. Palgrave worked as a missionary in Southern India and in Syria for some years.
In 1862 and 1863 he made a journey across Arabia for
the purpose of ascertaining missionary possibilities in
the peninsula and also as a secret agent for his employer, Napoleon III. He traveled as a Syrian Christian doctor and his greatest protection from Wahhabi
fanatics was his familiarity with Arabic language and
manners. His book, Narrative of a Year's Journey
through Central and Eastern Arabia, describes these
adventures. Finding mission work in Arabia impracti-
cal, Palgrave returned to England where he joined the
British diplomatic service and severed his ties with
the Jesuits. Palgrave's diplomatic missions sent him
to various parts of Africa and the Far East, the ease
with which he learned language helping him in diplomatic work as it had earlier helped with missionary
work. He married Katherine Simpson in 1868.

PELLY, COLONEL LEWIS. Resident in the Persian Gulf,
who went to Riyadh to see the Saudi ruler in 1864-
1865. Pelly desired to negotiate with the Saudi family
for help in suppression of piracy in the Persian Gulf,
but because of the unstable political situation in Riyadh
remained only three days.

PERIPLUS OF THE ERYTHRAEAN SEA   see ERYTHRAEAN
PERIPLUS

PERSIAN GULF. An arm of the Indian Ocean that extends
from the Straits of Hormuz northwestward to the Mesopotamian lowlands. The Persian Gulf separates the
peninsula of Arabia from Iran. Also called the Arabian Gulf.

PETROLEUM PRODUCTION   see OIL PRODUCTION

PETROMIN. General Petroleum and Mineral Authority, a state corporation set up by Royal Decree within the Saudi Ministry of Petroleum and Mineral Resources to participate in the development of petroleum and mineral interests in the Kingdom, and to distribute oil products within Saudi Arabia. The director of Petromin is the Minister of Petroleum and Mineral Resources and members include the Governor of SAMA, and the Deputy Minister of Finance.

PHILBY, HARRY ST. JOHN BRIDGER (1885-1960). English explorer and diplomat who spent many years in Saudi Arabia. An assistant to Sir Percy Z. Cox who was political resident from 1904, stationed at Bushire in Iran across the Persian Gulf from Arabia. Sent by Cox on a mission to Ibn Saud in 1917, Philby became a firm friend of the Saudi monarch. After the war and a period with the British Foreign Service in Transjordan, Philby resigned and became a business man at Jedda. He eventually joined the Moslem faith and in 1930 made a pilgrimage to Mecca. Philby made a number of geographical explorations in Arabia, especially in the Rub al Khali area, and he has written extensively on Arabian matters, history, geography, and contemporary social and political life.

PHOENIX DACTYLIFERA see DATE PALM

PICOT, GEORGES see SYKES-PICOT AGREEMENT

PILGRIM ROAD. The forty-seven miles from Jedda to Mecca, so called because most pilgrims for Mecca disembark at Jedda.

PITTS, JOSEPH. An enslaved Englishman who claimed to have visited Mecca in the latter part of the seventeenth century. The authenticity of his account has been questioned.

PLAIN OF SIBILA. Area in Sudair, north of Riyadh between Zilfi and Artiwiya where the Saudi and rebel Ikhwan forces met in 1929. The Ikhwan were crushingly defeated and their leaders either killed or captured.

POSTAL SERVICE. The postal system is primarily a post World War II phenomenon in Saudi Arabia. In 1970, there were approximately 400 post offices in the king-

dom and some 1,400 villages served on thirty-five de-
livery routes. Mail boxes (primarily in large cities)
are estimated at some tens of thousands. In 1969,
84.1 tons of domestic and 167.3 tons of foreign mail
were flown in and out of the Dhahran International Airport. Saudi Arabia is a member of the Universal Postal Union and issues stamps, including commemorative
issues. The first Saudi stamps appeared in the Nejd
in 1925, a combined Nejd-Hejaz stamp came out in
1926, but first stamps for the Kingdom as a whole
were issued only in 1934.

There were earlier stamps in Arabia, however, the
Hashimite rulers of the Hejaz produced stamps beginning in 1916.

PROPHETS MOSQUE   see MEDINA, PROPHETS MOSQUE

PUBLIC LIBRARIES. A Department of Libraries was formed
in the Kingdom in 1960. As of 1970 a number of Public Libraries had been established at Hofuf, Dammam,
Buraida, Unaiza, Shaqra, and Riyadh. Libraries are
planned for other cities including both Mecca and Medina.

In addition, the University of Riyadh has a library
of some 50,000 volumes.

-Q-

QADI (Qadhi). In Saudi Arabia and other Islamic countries,
a religious judge. In Saudi Arabia these judges are
Sunni and usually members of the Hanbali School.

QALAMAT. In Arabic, a drilled well.

QARMATIANS. A violent Moslem sect of the late ninth century, originating in the Hasa and in Bahrein. The
Qarmatians gained control of a large part of Arabia
and took Mecca in 930 A.D., briefly capturing the sacred Black Stone of the Kaaba and carrying it off to
their capital near Hofuf. See also ARABIA, HISTORY
OF--ISLAMIC PERIOD.

QASIDA. The ode, a major poetical form in Arabic. Qasida
are recorded from pre-Islamic times, in fact the Seven
Muallaqat, recognized today as brilliant poetical works,
are supposed to have been awarded prizes at the Ukaz

fair, probably in the early or mid-sixth century A. D.

QASIM.   The district Al Qasim extends along the course of
the Wadi Rumma and into the northern part of the Sirr
Desert.   The most important towns of the district are
Unaiza and Buraida.

QASSIS.   The tasselled sedge that grows on the side of sand
dunes in Arabia.   Cyperus conglomeratus.

QATABAN.   Kingdom of southern Arabia in the first millin-
eum B. C.   In its later periods, along with Ausan and
Hadhramaut, this civilization was referred to as Himyaritic rather than Minaean or Sabaean, from the powerful
tribe of Himyar.

QATAR.   Peninsula in the Persian Gulf that, as an independent Sheikdom, joined the United Nations in 1971 as its
smallest member.   Population of Qatar is some 55, 000.
Qatar shares with Saudi Arabia, Bahrein, and Kuwait
a great wealth of oil, producing in 1969 149 million
barrels of crude oil.

QATIF, TREATY OF   see TREATY OF QATIF

QIDD (Jidd).   Local Arabic name for a variety of barracuda
found in the Persian Gulf.

QIRSH AMIRI.   The eleventh part of a riyal, established by
the Saudi government in 1928.   In 1936 the qirsh amiri
was replaced by a qirsh saudi, used only for accounting purposes.

QIRSH DARIJ.   The "common qirsh, " a coin worth a twenty-
second part of the riyal, established in 1928 as part
of a monetary reform in Saudi Arabia.   The qirsh is
still used and qirsh coins are in circulation.   Half and
quarter qirsh coins were once minted but have now
been withdrawn.
In 1960, the qirsh was changed so that twenty of
these coins would equal one riyal and each qirsh was
further subdivided into five halala, thus effecting a
decimal coinage for Saudi Arabia.

QIRSH SAUDI.   A denomination used for accounting purposes
and worth two common qirsh (qirsh darij).

QIYAS.   Analogy.   A basis for the superstructure of Islamic
    dogma and law recognized by the Sunni Moslems along
    with the Koran, the hadith, and the ijma.   Analogy al-
    lows Moslem theologians to treat new situations (ones
    perhaps not even known in Muhammad's time) by ana-
    logic comparison with old situations.   For example the
    prohibition against alcoholic drink can, by analogy, be
    extended to drugs or even tobacco.   The Hanbali school
    of Sunni Islam tended to reject the concept of analogy
    as do their modern offshoots, the highly conservative
    Wahhabis.

QIZAN   see ASIR

QUNFIDA.   Small coastal town in central Asir.

QURAISH   see ARABIA, HISTORY OF--ISLAMIC PERIOD

                                 -R-

RACES IN SAUDI ARABIA.   The basic population of Saudi
    Arabia (as is true of the peninsula as a whole) is a
    Mediterranean variety of Caucasian.   There has been
    over the centuries a considerable admixture of Negroid
    elements but because of complex tribal and clan mar-
    riage customs, leading to a virtual caste system in
    some cases, the genetic picture is rather confused.
    Highest incidence of Negroid phenotypic features appear
    in the Tihama, while the Bedouin, especially in the
    Nejd tends to the more classic "Mediterranean" type,
    though there is Negroid admixture in some areas.   In
    a large band from Khaibar and the Shammar area to
    the Wadi Dawasir there are extensive Bedouin Negro
    mixes, the Banu Khudhair.   A low caste group called
    the Suluba or Slaib, who are mainly craftsmen and
    hunters, are found in eastern Saudi Arabia.   They dif-
    fer somewhat genetically from the Bedouin proper be-
    cause of the endogamous marriage rules but have not
    been very extensively studied.
        Racial prejudice in the western sense seems to be
    absent in Saudi Arabia.   The strict marriage rules
    among upper class people are actually related to class
    and lineage rather than to race.

RADIO.   In charge of the Ministry of Education there are at
    present major broadcasting stations at Jedda, Riyadh

and Dammam, both for long and short wave broadcast.
The Jedda station broadcasts to the outside world.

RAFHA. Town in extreme northern Saudi Arabia. Rafha is
   a pump station on the Trans-Arabian Pipeline system.

RAHATH. Small flowering plant found in the Aflaj area of
   Saudi Arabia. Eremobium agyptiacum.

RAHMA, MOUNTAIN OF (Jabal al Rahmah). A rocky hill
   standing on the northern end of the Plain of Arafat
   near Mecca. Rahma is one of the important spots in
   the ceremonies of the Hajj or Pilgrimage to Mecca.

RAILROADS see TRANSPORTATION IN SAUDI ARABIA

RAMADAN, FAST OF. A religious duty of all Moslems is
   fasting and general abstinence during the daylight hours
   of Ramadan, the ninth month of the Islamic year. Traditionally, the fast begins at that moment of dawn when
   a black thread can be distinguished from a white thread,
   and continues till sundown. The last ten days of Ramadan are considered especially holy. The month ends
   with the feast of the Breaking of the Fast (Id al Fitr),
   one of the great ceremonies of Islam. This feast lasts
   through the first three days of Shawwal, the tenth
   month of the year.

RAMLA. Term used in southern Arabia for a sand desert,
   equivalent to Nafud.

RAS. Arabic word meaning cape (of land) or peninsula.

RAS TANURA. City in northeast Saudi Arabia some twenty-
   five airline miles north of Dhahran and deep sea har-
   bor for oil shipments. The port of Ras Tanura was
   opened to oil tankers in 1939, the first ship to call
   being the D. G. Schofield on May 1, 1939. Ras
   Tanura has a population of approximately 20,000. It
   is located on the tip of a long narrow peninsula of the
   same name.

RASHID FAMILY. The Emirs of Hail and ruling family in
   the Jabal Shammar during the nineteenth and early
   twentieth century. Subject to the Saudis in the early
   part of the nineteenth century, the Rashidi by mid-
   century had achieved virtual independence. The rise

of the house to power in eastern Arabia began with
tragedy; in 1866 Talal ibn Abdulla, Amir at Hail, committed suicide and was succeeded by Mitab ibn Abdulla,
his brother. Two years later, in 1868, sons of Talal
murdered Mitab and one of them, Bandar ibn Talal took
the Amirate. Still another brother of Mitab, Muhammad ibn Abdulla ibn Rashid, was in Riyadh at the time
and escaped. In 1872 he returned and killed his nephew
Bandar, and all of Bandar's brothers except one, a
child named Naif. An infant son of Bandar by a former wife of Mitab was also spared and this son, Abdul
Aziz, eventually succeeded Muhammad.

Under Muhammad the house of Rashid reached its
greatest extent and power. At his death in 1897 the
house of Rashid controlled much of the Nejd.

Under Muhammad's nephew, Abdul Aziz ibn Mitab
ibn Rashid, who was about thirty years old on assuming the amirship, the fortunes of the family went down
drastically. Ibn Saud retook Riyadh in 1902 and in the
subsequent years slowly bit into Rashidi controlled territory in the Nejd. In 1906, Abdul Aziz ibn Mitab ibn
Rashid was killed in a skirmish. His son, Mitab ibn
Abdul Aziz was murdered the following year by Sultan
ibn Hamud. A year later, in January, 1908 Sultan in
turn was murdered by his two brothers, Saud and
Faisal, Saud becoming the new ruler at Hail. In 1909,
however, Saud, the youngest son of Abdul Aziz ibn
Mitab, was restored to the throne in Hail by two members of an influential family in the Jabal Shammar
area, Hamud ibn Subhan and Zamil ibn Subhan. Saud
was assassinated in turn in 1920 and a grandson of
Abdul Aziz ibn Mitab named Abdulla ascended the
throne. The following year the city of Hail fell to the
Saudi ruler and the Rashidi dynasty was extinguished.

RAUNKIAER, BARCLAY (1888-1915). A Danish geographer
and explorer, son of the botanist, Professor Christen
Raunkiaer and the authoress, Ingeborq Raunkiaer. In
1911 Raunkiaer was sent by the Royal Danish Geographical Society on a collecting and exploring expedition to
east central Arabia. Granted permission by the Turkish government, the nominal overlords of Arabia,
Raunkiaer traveled via Constantinople and Baghdad,
Basra and Zober, to Kuwait, reaching the latter area
at the end of January, 1912. From Kuwait Raunkiaer
traveled with a camel caravan into the interior of Arabia, leaving on February 24, 1912. He went first to

Buraida just east of the Jabal Shammar and then to
Riyadh, which only a few years before had been reoc-
cupied by Abdul Aziz Ibn Saud. The latter was away
on a raid at the time Raunkiaer visited the Saudi capital, but on March 28, 1912 the young Dane was given
an audience with Abdul Rahman, the father of Abdul
Aziz.
From Riyadh, Raunkiaer went eastward to Hofuf and
then, with an escort of Turkish soldiers, to the Arabian Sea coastal town of Ajer (al Ugair), reaching there
on April 12.
The expedition of Barclay Raunkiaer was intended to
find a base for a much more ambitious expedition into
the southern deserts of Arabia, an expedition that was
to have had commercial aspects (the discovery of oil
sources) as well as scientific ones. This expedition
never was held, indeed Raunkiaer was ill during most
of his trip and failed to penetrate beyond the Wadi
Hanifa area. His account is valuable for the information that it gives about Kuwait in the pre-oil period
and for descriptions of the Wadi Hanifa towns.
Raunkiaer published an account of his journey upon
his return to Denmark and in 1916 the Arab Bureau in
Cairo translated this into English under the title
Through Wahhabiland on Camel-Back. A more recent
English edition was published in 1969 with an introduction and notes by Gerald de Gaury.

RAWDAT MOHANNA. Battle fought between King Ibn Saud
and the Rashidi forces near Buraida in the month of
Shawwal, A.H. 1324 (late fall, 1906).

RAWIE. A rawie is a person attached to a poet, who mem-
orizes verbatim the verse of that poet as it is composed, and thereby himself, learns the poetic trade.
This symbiotic relationship was important during the
time when most of the population was illiterate and
there was no other method to record the spoken word.
Some rawies specialized in genealogies and were the
encyclopedias of their time.

RED CRESCENT SOCIETY. In the Islamic world the equivalent of the Red Cross in western Society. The Red
Crescent Society in Saudi Arabia is a quasi-government
organization. In 1969 some 135 health personnel including thirteen physicians were on the Red Crescent
staff.

REINAUD, JOHN LEWIS. Assistant to the British Resident
in Basra who took refuge in Kuwait during the political
unrest in Iraq from 1793 to 1796. Following a Wahhabi
attack on Kuwait, Reinaud was sent to Diriya to rees-
tablish Wahhabi friendship.

RELIGION IN SAUDI ARABIA. By far the greater group of
Saudi Arabians are Sunni Moslems and of these, most
belong, at least nominally, to the conservative Wahhabi
or Unitarian interpretation of the Hanbali school. There
are Shia groups especially in the Hasa and in the extreme southwest of the kingdom. There are no native
Jews or Christians, though some thousands of Christians
are employed by the oil industry, mainly by ARAMCO.
Non-Moslems are not allowed in the holy cities of Mecca and Medina but members of the Islamic community
of whatever sect are welcome as pilgrims. See also
ISLAM.

RHOADES, RALPH O. Geologist sent by Gulf Oil Corporation to examine and map Bahrein for oil in 1927.

RIAL see RIYAL

RIDDA (Apostasy). The rebellion of several tribes following
the death of the Prophet Muhammad. Various tribes,
especially the Banu Hanifa (Hanifah) of south central
Arabia, denied owing allegiance to the successor of
Muhammad, the first Caliph, Abu Bakr. The latter
sent one of his key military leaders, Khalid ben al
Walid, to quell the rebellion which was led by a member of the Hanifa tribe named Musailima. In 633 a
major battle was fought at Akraba in central Arabia
and the Hanifa were defeated, Musailima being killed.

RIM. Arabian name for the large white gazelle found in the
Rub al Khali area.

RIMRAM. A heliotrope that grows in the sand hollows in the
Rub al Khali area. Heliotropium Rotschyi (Bunge)
Gürke.

RIYADH. Capital of Saudi Arabia and also capital of the
Nejd province. The city of Riyadh is some 480 miles
northeast of Mecca and is about 250 miles west of the
Persian Gulf. It is at an altitude of some 5000 feet.
The founding date of Riyadh is unknown but in medi-

eval times it was a stopping point on the main road between Iran and Mesopotamia and Mecca. Riyadh and
the surrounding area formed an extensive oasis that
has long produced large amounts of dates and cereals.
Riyadh became very quickly associated with the Wahhabi religious movement. When Muhammad Ibn Abdul
Wahhab, the founder of the movement was forced to
leave Hanifa, he was welcomed to Dariya, half a day's
journey further south in the Hanifa, by Muhammad ibn
Saud. This not only began the close relationship between the Saud house and the religious reformation of
Wahhabism but since Dahham ibn Dawwas, the governor of Riyadh, proved hostile to the new movement, it
led to a long drawn-out struggle between the two nearby districts.
    After a long struggle Dahham fled the city and it
was taken in 1773 or 1774 by Abdul Aziz Ibn Saud, son
of Muhammad ibn Saud and ardent follower of Wahhabism. From that date the city was strongly associated
with both the Wahhabi movement and with the Saud
family.
    In the late nineteenth century Riyadh was, for a
short time, overrun by the Rashid family of Hail, and
the Saud family was forced to flee to Kuwait. In 1902,
however, a young member of the Saud family, Abdul
Aziz ibn Abdul Rahman al Saud, who was to become
King Ibn Saud of Saudi Arabia, took the city and made
it his headquarters for conquest of the peninsula. With
the ascension of Ibn Saud's son, King Saud, in 1953,
the government offices at Jedda on the Red Sea coast
were moved to Riyadh.
    The city as well as being the seat of government,
contains the Jamida Mosque, a center of the Wahhabi
sect. The population of Riyadh is estimated (as of
1965) at 225,000. A railroad connects Riyadh with
Dhahran on the Persian Gulf and a motor road runs
from Jedda on the Red Sea, through Mecca, to Ash
Shagra (where a minor road runs northwest to Hail),
Riyadh, Hofuf, and on to the coast of the Persian Gulf.

RIYADH, UNIVERSITY OF. The major institution of higher
    learning in Saudi Arabia. The University was founded
    in 1957 having originally a Faculty of Arts. In subse-
    quent years Faculties of Science, Engineering, Phar-
    macy, Education, Commerce, Agriculture and Medicine
    have been added. In 1957 enrollment was twenty-one
    students, in 1965 this had risen to 1029 male and sixty-

one female students. In 1969-1970 the University had
2680 men and 219 women, a total of 2899 students.
  The Faculty of Arts in the University includes the
departments of history, geography, Arabic and English.
Persian and Latin are also taught and the B. A., M. A.,
and Ph. D. degree are offered. The Faculty of Sciences
includes departments of physics, mathematics, chemis-
try, botany, zoology, and geology, offering the B. S.,
M. S., and Ph. D. The Faculties of Pharmacy and
Commerce also offer the Ph. D. degree while the Faculty of Engineering, Agriculture and Education have
the bachelor's degree with qualification especially for
advanced study abroad. The Faculty of Medicine offers a bachelor's degree in medicine and surgery (the
equivalent of an American M. D. degree).
  Each regular student in the University receives a
monthly stipend from the national government of approximately $77. 00.

RIYAL. The standard of currency in Saudi Arabia. The
riyal or rial is valued at 4. 5 to the dollar, a single
riyal being worth about twenty-two cents. The modern
riyal was established as a currency base in 1928 with
the silver riyal pegged at one tenth of a British
sovereign. The riyal was divided into eleven quirsh
amiri and each of these was split into two qirsh darij.
The riyal was reissued in 1936 as a coin of 11. 66
grams, divided into twenty-two qirsh darij, the qirsh
amiri however being replaced with a unit used in accounting but never coined, called the qirsh saudi.
Half riyal and quarter riyal coins were also issued in
the 1930's, and half and quarter qirsh coins were also
issued, though these have since been withdrawn from
circulation.
  The Saudi sovereign, a gold coin worth forty riyals
was issued in 1952. Paper currency has been issued
from 1953. In 1960 the value of the riyal was fixed
at its present level.

RUALA (Ruwalla). A branch of the Anaiza tribe whose pas-
torage extend from the Syrian Desert south to Nejd.
The Ruala was conquered by Ibn Saud following the fall
of the Rashids in 1921.

RUB AL KHALI (The Empty Quarter). The great desert of
southeast Arabia. Because of the configuration of the
landforms of southern Arabia with steep hills that trap

monsoon rains, and because it lies beyond the range of
Mediterranean winter rains, the Rub al Khali is one of
the dryer areas of the earth.

RUMMA, WADI see NEJD

RUWALLA see RUALA

-S-

SABA. An early state in the Yemen area of southern Arabia beginning perhaps before 500 B.C. The Saba or
Sabaean state traded with the African Horn area and
colonized Abyssinia. Saba sea power gave her control
of the Straits of Bab al Mandab (the southern outlet of
the Red Sea). Eventually Saba absorbed the nearby rival state of Main. The kings of this augmented state
were called mukarribs and combined political and religious functions. The capital of Saba-Main was at
Marib in the Yemen hills, at an elevation of nearly
4000 feet and was famous both for its beautiful buildings
and for the elaborate water control systems. See also
ARABIA, HISTORY OF--EARLY PERIOD.

SABAEAN see SABA

SABLA, BATTLE OF see SIBILA, BATTLE OF

SADLIER, CAPTAIN G. F. An English officer in India service, who in 1819 crossed Arabia from east to west in
an effort to interview Ibrahim Pasha.

SAHBA, WADI see NEJD

SAHIH (The genuine). This collection of hadith under the
title of Kitab al jami as Sahih was made by al Bukhari
in the ninth century A.D. From a corpus of more
than 200,000 hadith (traditional statements or sayings
that date back to the life and times of the Prophet and
make up the Sunna), Bukhari chose less than three
thousand as authentic. Another group of hadith also
conventionally referred to as the Sahih was made by
the scholar, Muslim, working about the same time as
Bukhari.

SALIM AL SUBHAN. A commander of Rashidi forces who

was in control at Riyadh in 1880's and early 1890's.

SALT PRODUCTION. The Saudi Ministry of Petroleum and
    Mineral Resources has estimated the kingdom's salt
    reserves at a minimum of 500 million tons. Commer-
    cially valuable salt is found on both the Arabian Gulf
    and Red Sea coasts and is an important factor in the
    economy of southern Asir.

SAMA see SAUDI ARABIAN MONETARY AGENCY

SAMSI. A queen of Arabia who was forced by the Assyrian
    king, Tiglathpileser III, to pay tribute in 734 B. C.
    after a Palestinian coalition against Assyria had col-
    lapsed. According to a fragmentary text of Tiglathpi-
    leser's reign, Samsi seems to have been the head of a
    powerful state, for she lost 1, 000 people, 30, 000 cam-
    els, 20, 000 cattle, and 5, 000 bundles of spice. Samsi
    fled for safety to the city of Bazu (an unidentified
    place) but being overcome with hunger and terrified by
    the superior Assyrian military machine she offered
    camels to Tiglathpileser and accepted a political over-
    seer. It is not clear exactly where Samsi's kingdom
    was but the mention of spices suggests that she had
    trade contacts with south Arabia.

SANA. City in central Yemen, and traditional capital of
    Yemen. Population is estimated at 50, 000. See also
    YEMEN.

SANAD. The chain of authorities that are necessary to au-
    thenticate a hadith, the process being referred to as
    isnad (going back). The most famous editor of hadith
    was al Bukhari, author of the Sahih. As a result of
    the investigations into each hadith, the strength or
    weakness of the chain of each hadith could be put into
    one of three main categories; sahih (authentic, genuine),
    where the chain back to Muhammad has no weak link;
    hasan (good) where there is only one link and daif
    (weak) where the chain is suspect.

SARA BINT AHMAD AL KABIR AL SUDAIRI. Mother of Ibn
    Saud and a member of the great Sudairi family that of-
    ten intermarried with the Saudi.

SARKAN, CAPE OF (Ras Sarkan). Cape at the southwestern
    side of the Strait of Hormuz which separates the waters

of the Persian or Arabian Gulf from those of the Gulf
of Oman.

SAUD, DYNASTY OF.
Mani al Muraidi: flourished ca. 1450.
Rabia ibn Mani: fl. latter half 1400's.
Musa ibn Rabia: fl. ca. 1500.
Ibrahim ibn Musa: fl. 1500's.
Markhan ibn Ibrahim: fl. 1500's.
Miqrin ibn Markhan: fl. 1600's.
Muhammad ibn Miqrin: d. 1694.
Saud ibn Muhammad ibn Miqrin: d. ca. 1725.
Muhammad ibn Saud: ruled 1726-1766.
Abdul Aziz I ibn Saud: ruled 1766-1803.
Saud II ibn Saud: ruled 1803-1814.
Abdulla ibn Saud: ruled 1814-1818.
Mushari ibn Saud: ruled 1819-1820.
Turki ibn Abdulla ibn Muhammad: ruled 1820-1834.
Faisal ibn Turki ibn Saud: ruled 1834-1838, 1843-1865.
Abdulla ibn Faisal: ruled Civil War Period.
Saud ibn Faisal: ruled 1865-1889.
Abdul Rahman ibn Faisal: ruled under Rashids 1889-
   1891.
Abdul Aziz ibn Rahman ibn Faisal al Saud: ruled 1902-
   1953 (as King of Arabia, 1932-1953).
Saud ibn Abdul Aziz: ruled 1953-1964.
Faisal ibn Abdul Aziz: ruled 1964- .

SAUD IBN ABDUL AZIZ.   Cousin of Ibn Saud and one of the
   Araif who rebelled against the Saudi ruled 1910-1912
   but later became a loyalist.

SAUD IBN ABDUL AZIZ IBN RASHID.   Rashidi ruler in Hail
   from 1909 to 1920.   In the latter year Saud was assassinated.   The following year the city fell to Ibn Saud
   of Riyadh.   See also RASHID FAMILY.

SAUD IBN FAISAL.   One of the sons of Faisal ibn Turki who
   struggled for a number of years with his brother Abdulla for the headship of the Saud family.   Saud controlled the Saudi house for the period 1871-1875 but in
   the latter year was killed in a border skirmish near
   Huraimila.

SAUD IBN HAMUD.   Ruler of Hail 1908-1909 following the
   murder of his brother Sultan ibn Hamud.   In 1909 Saud
   was replaced by Saud ibn Abdul Aziz, the rightful

Rashidi ruler.

SAUD IBN JILUWI. Longterm governor of the Hasa and
   kinsman of Ibn Saud.

SAUD II IBN SAUD. Ruler during the first expansionist
   period of Saudi Arabia. Saud was made heir to the
   throne of Arabia in 1788 by his father Abdul Aziz I
   ibn Saud. On the death of Abdul Aziz in 1803, Saud
   over the next decade achieved a rather shaky and uncertain control over the Hejaz, a control that was lost
   after his death in 1814.

SAUD, KING OF SAUDI ARABIA (Saud ibn Abdul Aziz ibn
   Abdul Rahman al Saud). Born in Kuwait in the early
   part of the year 1902 (a few months before his father,
   Ibn Saud, retook Riyadh) Saud was the third son of Ibn
   Saud. Saud's mother was the daughter of the chief of
   the important Kalid tribe of the Hasa. More insular
   than his younger brother Faisal, Saud played relatively
   little part in Arabian politics till 1925 when, after the
   Saudi conquest of the Hejaz, he was made viceroy of
   Nejd. The battle of Sibila (Sabla) in 1929, which
   ended the Ikhwan rebellion, saw Saud actively in the
   field. In 1933 Saud was named Crown Prince and
   joined Faisal in the war against Yemen the following
   year, a war that led to the Saudi annexation of Najran
   and Yam. In 1935 Crown Prince Saud made his first
   trip to Europe (he was to visit the United States in
   1947 at the invitation of President Truman).
      In 1953 Saud was made President of the newly
   formed Council of Ministers and that same year became King of Saudi Arabia following the death of Ibn
   Saud.
      Saud's term as king was not entirely successful, due
   in part to recurring illness, and in part to a somewhat
   unsophisticated approach to complex problems of the
   modern world. Nevertheless, Saud pressed for the
   modernization of Saudi Arabia, being especially interested in education and medicine.
      On November 2, 1964, Saud, at the request of the
   Saudi Council of Ministers, the royal family and the
   Supreme Council of Religious Leaders, relinquished the
   throne to Faisal, the formal abdication taking place in
   January, 1965. Saud died in Athens, Greece, on the
   23rd of February, 1969.

SAUDI ARABIA. Except for the entries below, material that
relates to modern Saudi Arabia will be found under their
own subject headings.

SAUDI ARABIA, ANNUAL BUDGET OF. The annual budgets
of Saudi Arabia, drawing mainly from oil subsidies,
have more than tripled over the decade 1960-1970. A
breakdown by year gives the following figures (in American currency):

1960-61	$ 392, 920, 000
1961-62	$ 476, 520, 000
1962-63	$ 539, 484, 000
1963-64	$ 590, 920, 000
1964-65	$ 684, 640, 000
1965-66	$ 871, 420, 000
1966-67	$1, 105, 500, 000
1967-68	$1, 086, 140, 000
1968-69	$1, 217, 810, 000
1969-70	$1, 312, 520, 000

SAUDI ARABIA, FLAG OF. The official Saudi flag has, on
a green field, a sword, and over the sword the words,
"There is no God but Allah and Muhammad is God's
Messenger."

SAUDI ARABIA, HISTORY OF. Although the Kingdom of
Saudi Arabia was not officially founded until 1932, its
roots go much deeper. For centuries the center and
source of Saudi power has been the Wadi Hanifa area
in east central Arabia. It was around 1450 when the
first member of the Saudi group, either a man named
Mani al Muraidi or his son, Rabia, brought a party to
settle in the Wadi Hanifa, apparently on estates owned
by his cousin, one Ibn Dira. The newcomers named
their new village Dariya after a suburb of Qatif, from
which they came. The family of Mani managed to
firmly establish themselves in the Wadi during the
course of the next century and a half. Under Rabia
and his son, Musa, the Mani family gradually expanded
over the central Hanifa area. In the early sixteenth
century Ibrahim ibn Musa consolidated these gains and
one of his sons, Abdul Rahman founded the settlement
of Dhurna (Durna) west of Dariya. Another son, Markhan, became the direct ancestor of the first Saud.
    The real rise of Saud power came in the early
eighteenth century. After a period of considerable confusion in which several families were struggling for

control of Dariya, Saud ibn Muhammad ibn Miqrin, at
some point before 1720, regained control of the city for
the lineage of Mani and became the eponymous founder
of the Saud dynasty. Saud died in 1725 and after a dynastic squabble was succeeded by a son, Muhammad
ibn Saud. This period saw the appearance of the reformer, Muhammad ibn Abdul Wahhab, who was born
in Ayaina in 1703 and who, in 1745, made a famous
alliance with Muhammad ibn Saud, whereby the Saud
family became supporters of Wahhabism.

In 1765 Abdul Aziz ibn Muhammad ibn Saud (Abdul
Aziz I ibn Saud) who was at the time forty-four years
old, inherited the Amirate of Dariya. He continued the
support of Wahhabism and gradually expanded his do-
main from the Wadi Hanifa, and solidified control over
the Hasa, by defeating the Banu Khalid in 1789-1790.
Muhammad ibn Abdul Wahhab died in 1792, his basic
reforms by this time being well established. Saudi
expansion continued and the Iraqi center of Karbala,
the important pilgrimage center of the Shiite sect, was
overrun in 1802. However, the following year Abdul
Aziz himself was assassinated in Dariya. A son, Saud
Ibn Abdul Aziz, continued the expansionist policies of
the Saudi state, overrunning the Hejaz and holding it
from 1803-1804 till 1812-1813 when a counter attack
by the Ottoman governor of Egypt, Muhammad Ali regained the area. Muhammad Ali continued eastward
into Nejd and occupied Dariya in 1818.

In the 1820's and 1830's the, then, Saudi rulers,
Turki ibn Abdulla and Faisal ibn Turki, attempted to
maintain themselves in the Nejd but civil wars and a
dynastic struggle, plus the continuing presence of the
Turks, prevented any large scale expansion of Saudi
power. From the mid 1850's to the 1880's the two
sons of Turki, Abdulla and Saud, struggled for power
and eventually Muhammad ibn Al Rashid of Hail entered the fight and annexed Riyadh. For a time Abdul
Rahman ibn Faisal, a younger brother of Abdulla and
Saud, controlled Riyadh under the Rashid amirs. In
1891, however, Abdul Rahman was forced to flee with
his family, including an eleven year old son who was
to be the famous Ibn Saud, twentieth century refounder
of Saudi Arabia. See IBN SAUD, KING AND FOUNDER
OF SAUDI ARABIA.

SAUDI ARABIA, KINGDOM OF. Composed of the old states
of Nejd, Hejaz, Asir, Hasa plus the southern and

northern desert area, Saudi Arabia has an area of
872, 722 square miles. It is enclosed on the west and
east by the Red Sea and the Persian Gulf. Bordering
Saudi Arabia on the north are the nations of Jordan,
Iraq, and Kuwait plus two neutral zones of disputed
territory. On the east, the kingdom is bordered by
Bahrein, Qatar, the Union of Arab Emirates, Muscat
and Oman, and on the south by Southern Yemen and
Yemen.
Various population figures are given for Saudi Arabia; a 1963 estimate is 7, 000, 000 but present population is considerably higher. The capital is Riyadh in
the Nejd, with embassies and Ministry of Foreign Affairs at Jedda on the Red Sea. See also under subject
headings.

SAUDI ARABIA, POLITICAL ORGANIZATION. Until the post
World War II period the Saudi Kingdom was ruled more
or less as a typical desert sheikdom. The conquest of
King Ibn Saud however, brought Saudi rule to much of
the Arabian peninsula and the exploitation of oil brought
wealth to the country and a more complex governmental
structure became necessary. A number of ministries
have been set up, especially in the post World War II
years, either as outgrowth of earlier bodies or as
completely new entities. The ministries with founding
dates are:
  Agriculture and Water, 1954
  Commerce and Industry, 1954
  Communications, 1953
  Defense and Aviation (originally Agency of Defense),
    1933-34 (includes National Guard)
  Education and Schools, 1953
  Finance and National Economy, 1933
  Foreign Affairs, 1930
  Health, 1951
  Information, 1963
  Interior, 1951
  Justice, 1960
  Labour and Social Affairs, 1961
  Petroleum and Mineral Resources, 1960
  Pilgrimage and Endowments, 1962
Other agencies include the Consultative Council, a
kind of legislative assembly for the Hejaz. There is
a separate labor department and an agency of Broad-
casting. In 1954, following the death of Ibn Saud, a
Council of Ministers of some fifteen members was

formed and this body has had a considerable effect on the policies of Saudi Arabia since that time.

The judiciary is independent and has local and appelate courts. The religious leaders are organized into the Ulema, headed by the Grand Mufti who is appointed by the King.

The country is divided into five administrative areas. Hejaz, Nejd, Asir, Northern Frontier Province, and the Eastern Province, (the old province of Hasa). The larger towns have municipal governments that supervise purely urban affairs.

The capital of Saudi Arabia is Riyadh, though Jedda on the Red Sea contains the foreign embassies and the Saudi Ministry of Foreign Affairs.

SAUDI ARABIA, RACES OF   see RACES OF SAUDI ARABIA

SAUDI ARABIA, RELIGION IN   see RELIGION IN SAUDI ARABIA

SAUDI ARABIAN MINING SYNDICATE, LTD.   The company that from 1934 to 1954 held a concession to exploit the Mahab Dhahab area mines.   In this twenty year period the company extracted some thirty million dollars in gold and silver.   See also MAHAB DHAHAB.

SAUDI ARABIAN MONETARY AGENCY (SAMA).   This agency was set up in 1952 by royal decree to reinforce the value of the Arabian riyal and to produce financial flexibility that would make funds available for economic growth and development in Saudi Arabia.   The agency's powers include the safeguarding and investing of funds, purchase and sale of gold and foreign currencies and the control and supervision of commerical banks in the nation.   Within the framework of SAMA, Saudi Arabia became the first Middle Eastern country (in 1960) to achieve complete convertibility of its currency.   The riyal, currently, enjoys 100% gold and foreign currency convertibility and its use has spread beyond the nation of Saudi Arabia, the small states along the Arabian Gulf now using the riyal as their official currency.

SAUDI GOVERNMENT RAILROADS   see TRANSPORTATION

SEALAND   see ARABIA, HISTORY OF--EARLY PERIOD

SEA WATER DESALINATION DEPARTMENT.   Formed as an

agency of the Ministry of Agriculture and Water in 1965, this department has charge of the various desalination projects in modern Saudi Arabia.   See also WATER RESOURCES AND DEVELOPMENT.

SHAFI.   Named after Muhammad ibn Idris ash Shafi who died ca. A. D. 820, one of the four Sunni schools of jurisprudence that appeared in the eighth and ninth centuries, A. D.   Rising from the Maliki school, the Shafi held that local time-honored traditions could be used.   When appeal to contemporary authority was necessary it need not be the theologians of Medina.

SHAKESPEAR, CAPTAIN W. H. I.   Arabic speaking British diplomatic liason officer to Ibn Saud during the first part of World War I.   Shakespear's mission was to promote the anti-Turkish (and anti-Rashid) feelings of the Sauds and cement British-Arab relations.   Although Shakespear was well versed in Saudi customs he refused to wear Arab dress and this fact probably caused his death during a battle between Ibn Saud and the Rashids on January 17, 1915.   In European dress Shakespear was an obvious target and fell to Rashidi force.

SHALMANESER III (Shulmanu-Asharedu, "The God Shulmanu Rules") (858-824 B. C.).   Assyrian King, son of Ashurnasirpal.   One of the documents of this king, a stele from Kurkh called the "monolithic inscription," contains an account of the battle of Karkar (854 or 853 B. C.) in the central Syrian Plains.   Here Shalmaneser fought a confederation that included a contingent of 1, 000 camels (presumably with riders) sent by Gindibu the Arabian.   This is the first known mention of an Arab in history.

SHAMMAR, MOUNTAINS OF   see JABAL SHAMMAR

SHAMMAR TRIBE.   The major group in the Jabal Shammar and in the area round Hail.   The Rashids were chiefs of the Shammar tribe.

SHAMSI.   Queen of Arabia.   See SAMSI.

SHARIA.   From Shar, "the way."   The law of Islam as revealed in the Koran and in the hadith.   The Sharia is especially important in Saudi Arabia because the Saudi Constitution is based on the Sharia.   All legal trans-

actions, even administrative codes and decisions, are
enacted within the framework of the Sharia.

SHARJAH. One of the former Trucial States, as of December, 1971; a member of the Union of Arab Emirates.
See also TRUCIAL COAST.

SHARR. Mountain peak in extreme northern Hejaz, 6398
feet in altitude.

SHEBA, QUEEN OF. Biblical Queen who visited Solomon.
If indeed a historical figure, Sheba may possibly have
been of the Sabaean kingdom in the southern part of
the Arabian peninsula, or, perhaps, from a more
northern Sabaean colony. See also ARABIA, HISTORY
OF--EARLY PERIOD.

SHEIK. Islamic traditional official usually at the tribal
level, also an honorary title for a family head or distinguished person.

SHERIF. A noble who descends from the Prophet Muham-
mad in the line of Hassan, the older son of Ali and
Fatima. The title of the rulers of Mecca was that of
Sherif of Mecca, called by Europeans the "Grand
Sherifs."
The last Sherif of Mecca, Ali ibn Hussein, son of
Hussein ibn Ali, who abdicated in his favor in October
of 1924, fled on the 22nd of December, 1925, follow-
ing the occupation of Jedda, on December 19th of that
year.

SHERIFS OF MECCA. The line of rulers of the city of
Mecca and surrounding countryside, at times including
much or all of the Hejaz. The family that ruled Mecca traced their descent from Hashim, a grandson of
Kosaiy, an early leader of the Quraish tribe of Mecca.
Hashim's son, Abdul Mutallib, became in turn the father of Abdulla Muhammad's father. Descendants of
this family through Fatima, daughter of Muhammad,
and Ali (the latter a son of Abu Talib, Muhammad's
father's brother) are referred to as Hashimites, especially those members who descended from Hassan,
the elder son of Ali and Fatima, the Hassiniya, or
Hassanite branch of direct line descent from Muhammad and from Hashim. From the beginning of the thir-
teenth century, rule in Mecca was in the hands of the

Bani Qitada who ruled with the titles of Emir (Prince specifically a descendant of Muhammad through Fatima) or Sherif till the area was overrun by Ibn Saud in 1925. At present, a member of this Qitada house is the Hashimite king of Jordan (Hussein) and until recently there were Hashimite kings of Iraq.

The following list is modified somewhat from de Gaury, 1951. It must be remembered that this is a traditional account.

Qitada ("Al Nibigha," of the Genius"; nicknamed Abu Aziz), of Yenbo, port of Medina, b. 1132, conqueror and thirteenth dynastic Emir of Mecca; descent--ibn Idris ibn Mutain ibn Abdul Karim ibn Muhammad (Abu Jaafar al Thaalab) ibn Abdulla al Akhbar ibn Muhammad al Thayir ibn Musa al Thani ibn Abdulla al Mahath ibn al Hassan al Muthanna ibn Hassan ibn Ali, son-in-law of the Prophet Muhammad.	1201-20
Hassan ibn Qitada.	1220-21
Rajih ibn Qitada.	1221-54
Idris ibn Qitada.	1253-54
Muhammad Abu Nomay.	1254-1301
Rumaitha.	1301-44
Ajlan.	1344-75
Ahmad ibn Ajlan.	1360-86
Muhammad ibn Ahmad.	1386
Anan ibn Mughaimis.	1386-87
Ali ibn Ajlan.	1387-94
Hassan ibn Ajlan.	1394-1425
Barakat ibn Hassan.	1425-55
Muhammad ibn Barakat.	1455-95
Barakat ibn Muhammad ibn Barakat.	1495-1524
Muhammad Abu Nomay ibn Barakat	1524-84
Hassan ibn Abi Nomay.	1584-1601
Idris ibn Hassan.	1601-24
Muhsin ibn Hussain.	1624-28
Ahmad ibn Talib al Hassan.	1628-30
Masoud ibn Idris.	1630
Abdulla ibn Hassan.	1630
Muhammad ibn Abdulla.	1631
Zaid ibn Muhsin.	1631-66
Saad ibn Zaid.	1666-71
Barakat ibn Muhammad.	1671-82
Said ibn Barakat.	1682-83
Ahmad ibn Zaid.	1669-71
	1684-87

Said ibn Saad.	1687-1716
Abdulla ibn Said.	1716-17
	1723-30
Ali ibn Said.	1717
Yahya ibn Barakat.	1717-19
	1721-22
Mubarak ibn Ahmad.	1719-21
	1723
Barakat ibn Yahya.	1722-23
Muhammad ibn Abdulla.	1730-32
	1732-34
Masoud ibn Said.	1732-33
	1734-52
Masaad ibn Said.	1750-58
	1759-70
Jaafar ibn Said.	1758-59
Abdulla ibn Said.	1770
Ahmad ibn Said.	1770
Abdulla ibn Hussein.	1770
Sarur ibn Masaad.	1773-88
(Abdul Muin ibn Said, 1788, for one day).	
Ghalib ibn Masaad.	1788-1813
Yahya ibn Sarur (Under control of	1813-27
Muhammad Ali Pasha of Egypt).	
Abdul Muttalib ibn Ghalib.	1827-28
	1852-56
	1880-81
Muhammad ibn Abdul Muin ibn Aun.	1828-36
Abdulla ibn Muhammad ibn Aun.	1858-77
Hussein ibn Muhammad ibn Aun.	1877-80
Abdulla ibn Muhammad ibn Aun	1879-80
(Abdulla Pasha).	1881-82
Aun al Rafiq ibn Muhammad ibn Aun.	1882-1905
Ali Ibn Abdulla ibn Muhammad ibn Aun.	1905-8
Hussein ibn Ali.	1908-24
Ali Ibn Hussein.	1924-25

SIBILA   see PLAIN OF SIBILA

SIBILA, BATTLE OF.   Battle between the loyalist forces of
   Ibn Saud and the rebellious Ikhwan in 1929.   The defeat
   of the Ikhwan led to the gradual political decline of
   this Wahhabi Brotherhood.   See also IKHWAN.

SILVER PRODUCTION.   At present relatively little silver
   mining is in progress in Saudi Arabia but a number of
   potential sites are known particularly in the triangle

formed by the sites of Dawadimi, Quwaiya and Holaiban in the plateau southwest of Riyadh and west of the Tuwaiq escarpment, an area that also contains gold and copper. The Directorate General of Petroleum and Mining Resources is in charge of plans for eventual silver exploitation.

SIMPSON, KATHERINE. Wife of William G. Palgrave, famous diplomat and writer on Saudi Arabia. See also PALGRAVE, WILLIAM G.

SINGING SANDS. A phenomenon of the Nafud, Rub al Khali and other places that a booming, musical sound is made as sand slides from the top of a dune to the bottom.

SIRAH. One of several works on the life of the Prophet Muhammad. The earliest known Sirah is that of Ibn Ishaq (died A.D. 768); however, we have this book in a later recension, that of Ibn Hisham (died A.D. 833).

SIRHAN, WADI. A large system of Wadis (including the Wadi Fajr) that drains large areas of the Jordanian-Saudi Arabian border.

SIRR DESERT. A north-south tongue of desert in Nejd extending south from the Shammar area west of and paralleling the northern Jabal Tuwaiq.

SLAVERY. Until recently slaves were openly bought and sold in Saudi Arabia, as in other parts of the peninsula. As early as 1936 King Ibn Saud made a somewhat ineffective attempt to control the trade in slaves by forbidding their importation by sea. In September, 1962, slavery was declared illegal, in large part because of policy decisions of Faisal. It may, however, be another generation before the last vestiges of slavery disappear from Saudi Arabia.

SOCOTRA. Large island off the southern coast of Arabia. Now a part of the People's Republic of Southern Yemen.

SOUTHERN YEMEN, PEOPLE'S REPUBLIC OF. A nation formed in 1967 from the Protectorate of South Arabia. Southern Yemen has about 112,075 square miles and has a population of perhaps 900,000. The national capital of Southern Yemen is Aden, which, with a pop-

ulation of 250,000, is also the largest city. The nation is bordered on the west and north by Yemen and
Saudi Arabia, on the east by Oman, and on the south
by the Indian Ocean and the Gulf of Aden. The island
of Socotra is included within its territories.

SUBAITI. The grouper, a food fish in the Persian Gulf.

SUBKHA. Salt flats, usually in low lying areas near the
sea. These always contain water, usually only a few
feet below the surface and may be lakes that have been
filled with sand. In some subkhas evaporation has
created layers of salt that can be mined.

SUDAIR. District north of Riyadh in the Wadi Rima region.
A center of early Ikhwan settlement.

SUDAIRI FAMILY. Important family from the Wadi Dawasir
area who have frequently intermarried with the Saudi.
The mother of Ibn Saud was a member of this group,
as was one of his important wives, and also the first
wife of King Faisal.

SULEIYIL. Oasis some fifty miles east of Dam, on the
Wadi Dawasir. Suleiyil has several villages and a
population of perhaps 2000 inhabitants plus Bedouins
who visit the oasis during the date harvest season.

SULTAN IBN BIJAD. Member of the Ataiba tribe and chief
of the Ikhwan town of Ghatghat. Sultan was leader of
the Saudi forces that overran Taif in September, 1924,
and were involved in the massacre there. Sultan was
an opponent of Ibn Saud in the Ikhwan uprising of 1929
and was captured in the battle of the Plain of Sibila.
He died shortly afterward in Riyadh.

SULTAN IBN HAMUD. Short time ruler of Hail (1907-1908)
after his murder of Mitab ibn Abdul Aziz. Sultan was
killed in turn by his brothers, Saud and Faisal. See
also RASHID FAMILY.

SULTANA BINT AHMAD AL SUDAIRI. First wife of King
Faisal of Saudi Arabia; a member of the important
Sudairi family.

SURRA, WADI see NEJD

SYKES, SIR MARK (1879-1919). British politician who par-
ticipated in the talks that led to a secret settlement
between Britain and France on the influence of their
respective countries in the post-World War I Near East.

SYKES-PICOT AGREEMENT. An agreement worked out in
1916 between Sir Mark Sykes of England and Georges
Picot of France which delineated French and British
zones of influence in Arabia and other parts of the
Near East.

-T-

TABAQAT. The compilation of Ibn Saad (died A.D. 845) on
the lives of companions of the Prophet Muhammad.

TAIF. An agricultural center on the escarpment some forty
miles east and south of Mecca. Taif was settled in
pre-Islamic times and throughout much of its long history has supplied Mecca with grain and other food-
stuffs. At an elevation of about 5500 feet, Taif has a
pleasant climate and is a chief resort area. Today,
Taif is a road junction, being on the main highway
from Mecca to Riyadh and also the terminus for a new
system of roads that reach south into Asir. An important landmark in Taif is the Abdulla ibn Abbas
Mosque. Present population of Taif is approximately
60,000. The nearby town of Hada, higher and even
more moderate in climate, is a favorite resort area.

TAIF, TREATY OF see TREATY OF TAIF

TAIMIYA (Taqi al Din Ahmad ibn Taimiya). Conservative
Moslem scholar of the Hanbali school who strongly
influenced the later Wahhabi school. Taimiya (1263-
1328) was born in Haran but spent most of his adult
life in Damascus.

TAIZ. The principal town of the highland area of Yemen,
population ca. 12,000. See also YEMEN.

TALAL IBN ABDULLA. Early Rashid amir who committed
suicide in rather mysterious circumstances. See also
RASHID FAMILY.

TAMIM TRIBE. The southern Nejdi tribal group to which

reformer Muhammad ibn Abdul Wahhab belonged.

TAPLINE   see TRANS-ARABIAN PIPE LINE COMPANY

TARAFA ABNUL ABD.   A pre-Islamic poet whose indiscretions lead to his early death at the age of twenty-seven. He made the mistake of ridiculing the King of Hira, a patron of both Tarafa and an uncle, also a poet.   The king showed no signs of displeasure and gave them each a document of award to be presented to the Governor of Bahrein.   Since neither could read, Tarafa's uncle consulted a scribe during the journey to Bahrein.   On his discovery that they were carrying their own death sentences he fled to Syria.   Since he failed to inform Tarafa of the contents, the latter continued the journey to his death.

TARUT ISLAND.   Small island between Dammam and Ras Tanura.   See also DARIN.

TATHLITH, WADI OF   see ASIR

TELEPHONES AND TELEGRAPHS.   Although telephone and telegraph-radiograph service really began only in post World War II times, Saudi Arabia, in 1970, had 28,000 telephone lines.   A project slated to finish in 1971 at cost of more than fifty million dollars will add thirteen automatic exchanges and 76,600 new lines in ten major cities.

Since the early 1960's there has been rapid development of telegraph services with the replacement of wire by wireless equipment, the installation of teleprinter equipment at major cities, use of underground cable (linking Jedda, Yanbu and Medina) and installation of telephone booths.   At present there are cable offices in all major cities.

Beginning in 1970 communication training schools opened at Jedda and at Riyadh, drawing assistance from specialists of the World Federation of Telephone and Wireless.

Phone and wire services is under the charge of the Ministry of Communications.

TELEVISION.   There has been great development of television in Saudi Arabia in recent years.   As of 1970 the nation had five stations, one at Riyadh, one serving Jedda, Mecca and Taif, one at Medina, one at Qasim and one at Dammam. The main Jedda station has relay stations at Mecca and Taif which could operate independently in case the Jedda equipment failed.

THAMUD. An ancient village site in the Hail area recently discovered by a Saudi Arabian archaeologist.

THESIGER, WILFRED. British explorer born in Addis Ababa in 1910 at a time when his father was British Minister in that city. Thesiger, in the period 1945-1950, traveled extensively in eastern and southern Arabia, especially in the Rub al Khali.

THOMAS, BERTRAM. In 1931, the first western explorer to cross the Rub al Khali, traveling from Salala on the Arabian Sea to Qatar.

TIHAMA. The narrow coastal strip that lies between the Red Sea and the edge of the Arabian plateau. The highland which extends from near the Gulf of Aqaba to Yemen and flanks the Tihama on the east rises gradually as one goes south, in Yemen reaching elevations of over 10,000 feet.
     The Tihama is sometimes divided into three sections corresponding to the three major political units of western Arabia. In the north there is the Tihama of Hejaz, to the south the Tihama of Asir and in southwest Arabia, the Tihama of Yemen. The Tihama is very dry, though water from the adjacent highlands can be tapped for use as in the case of Jedda. Heat in the Tihama area is extremely oppressive at certain times of the year.

TRANS-ARABIAN PIPE LINE COMPANY (Tapline). A pipe line for crude oil built by ARAMCO (q.v.) beginning in 1949 from the Dhahran, Abqaiq Ras Tanura area to Sidon in Lebanon. The line runs through extreme northern Saudi Arabia and crosses Jordan and southern Syria.

TRANSPORTATION IN SAUDI ARABIA. Systems of transportation in Saudi Arabia have been greatly spurred in post World War times. In the fiscal year 1969-1970 the kingdom spent $118,580,000 in various road and port projects, $81,280,000 on air facilities, and $8,970,000 on railroads. Special concentration has been put on major roads. In 1962 there were 1,950

miles of trunk roads in Saudi Arabia and by 1969 this
mileage had increased to 4, 600 miles. Agricultural
roads as such began to be constructed in the year
1964-1965 with the completion of 900 miles during that
period. By 1969 there were nearly 1, 100 miles of agricultural roads.

In the year 1969 a total of 8, 349 ships called at
Saudi Arabian ports, more than a third of them (2889)
at the eastern oil port of Ras Tanura. For the Red
Sea ports, Jedda handled the most ships (1, 327) re-
flecting the pilgrimage situation and general trade de-
mands of the Hejaz.

Saudi Arabian airline traffic has showed drastic increase in the period 1960 to 1970. In terms of seat
miles produced, the rise has been from approximately
160, 000, 000 to over 700, 000, 000. There are major
airports at Medina, Jedda, Riyadh, and Dhahran, the
latter three being international airports. Especially
impressive is the innovative architecture of the airport
terminal at Dhahran, though the Jedda airport handles
most of both incoming and outgoing passenger traffic
(approximately 30% and 40% respectively in 1969).

In 1904-1908 the Turkish government, with German
technical help, completed a railroad from Damascus
to Medina, but this road was destroyed by British and
Arab forces under Lawrence of Arabia during the First
World War. Though it was put back in service in 1918
and used sporadically till 1924, it has since been deserted. In the late 1940's King Ibn Saud decided to
commission a railroad from Dammam to Riyadh and
with ARAMCO help this project was completed in 1951,
a distance of 370 miles. This project, called the
Saudi Government Railroad, was economically successful until the completion of paved roads from the coast
to Riyadh beginning in 1962 offered alternate and cheap-
er transportation. Between 1960 and 1969 the amount
of freight hauled on the Saudi railroad declined from
over 140, 000, 000 ton miles to some 27, 000, 000 ton
miles. Actual number of passengers carried increased
during this period from 58, 000 in 1960 to 115, 000 in
1969 and actual tonnage carried from 721, 000 to
941, 000. These latter figures represent the overall
increase in personal and economic activity in the eastern part of Arabia.

TREATY OF JEDDA. Treaty of May 20, 1927, by which
    the British recognized the Saudi Kingdoms of the Hejaz
    and Nejd.

TREATY OF QATIF. An agreement reached in 1915 whereby the British recognized Saudi hegemony in the Nejd
and in the Hasa.

TREATY OF TAIF. A treaty signed in May, 1934, between
Saudi Arabia and Yemen which delimited the Saudi, Yemen boundary following the Saudi-Yemeni war of the
previous year.

TRUCIAL COAST. In the early nineteenth century piracy
was almost the only means of support for certain
sheikdoms on the Persian Gulf. In 1835 the British
brought a halt to the piracy by establishing the Trucial
Coast, made up of small states on the Gulf, Abu Dhabi,
Dubai, Umm al Quwain, Sharjah, Ajman, Fujairah, and
Ras al Khaimah. These states were under the protection of the British Political Resident in the Gulf and
when the British withdrew in December of 1971 all but
Ras al Khaimah agreed to unite for mutual benefit.
This nation, which immediately announced that it wished
to join the United Nations, calls itself the Union of
Arab Emirates. The six member nations vary greatly
in size and national income but all are linked by a
national language, Arabic, and the faith of Islam. See
also each state individually.

TUMADHIR AL KHANSAA. The greatest poetess of early
Moslem times. After embracing Islam, Tumadhir, ac-
cording to tradition, recited her poetry for Muhammad.
In 646 her four sons were killed at the battle of
Qadisiya at which the Persians were defeated by the
Moslems.

TURKI IBN ABDULLA IBN MUHAMMAD. A cousin of Abdulla I ibn Saud who escaped the seige of Diriya in
1818. Turki rallied the Saudi forces and after some
initial failures managed to take Riyadh in 1824. Turki
overran Nejd and parts of the Hasa but was assasi-
nated at Riyadh in early May, 1834 while emerging
from Friday prayers at a mosque. His assassin was
a cousin, Mishari ibn Abdul Rahman. Turki's son,
Faisal ibn Turki who was, at the time, in the Hasa
returned to Riyadh and recaptured the city, killing
Mishari.

TURUBA. Town some eighty miles southwest of Taif in the
Hejaz. Turuba was the site of a crushing defeat suf-

fered by Hussein, the Hashimite Sherif of Mecca. In May, 1919, Hejazi forces under Abdulla ibn Hussein were largely destroyed by Ibn Saud, thus relieving a threat to Khurma and giving the Saudis a foothold in Hejaz.

TUWAIQ MOUNTAINS. A Jurassic limestone escarpment running roughly north and south for some five hundred miles. Elevation above sea level of this escarpment averages 2800 feet and has a maximum elevation of some 3500 feet. The Jabal Tuwaiq lies to the west and especially to the south of Riyadh and on its eastern side are several oasis areas, including Hauta, Hariq and Aflaj.

TWITCHELL, KARL S. An American engineer sent to Saudi Arabia in 1942 as a member of the first American agricultural mission there. The purpose of the mission was to examine the agricultural and irrigation possibilities of Saudi Arabia and make recommendations on specific methods of development. Twitchell was instrumental in establishing the gold-mining operations in the Hejaz under the direction of the Saudi Arabian Mining Syndicate. He was also involved in the development of oil resources that eventually became the basis of the present oil industry in eastern Saudi Arabia.

-U-

UKAZ. Town between Mecca and Taif where a merchant's fair and poetical competition was held annually. In the year A. D. 620 Muhammad met a number of men from Yathrib and so impressed them that two years later he was invited to make Yathrib his home.

ULEMA. Religious scholars who are learned in the Sharia. Often used as a collective name for religious jurists. Plural of alim.

UMANIYA. A breed of camel, produced by the Al Murra tribe of the Rub al Khali area, that is famous for its endurance. The Umaniya breed is able to maintain high average speed with little or no water for several days. It is, however best suited for moderate weight of cargo.

UMM AL QAWAIN. One of the Trucial Coast states that, in
    1971, joined the Union of Arab Emirates. See also
    TRUCIAL COAST.

UMRAH. A lesser pilgrimate than the Hajj which may be
    made at any time of the year.

UNAIZA. An important center in the al Qasim district about
    half way between Riyadh and Hail. Unaiza and its sis-
    ter city Buraida, some fifteen miles to the north are
    on the main roads leading north to Iraq. At present
    the road system westward to Medina and the Hejaz is
    being developed. Population of Unaiza is estimated at
    30, 000.

UNION OF ARAB EMIRATES. Union of various Trucial
    Coast states formed in December, 1971. See also
    TRUCIAL COAST and individual states.

UNITARIANISM. The Wahhabi reform movement. See also
    MUWAHHIDUN; MUHAMMAD IBN ABDUL WAHHAB.

UYAINA see AYAINA

-W-

WADI. A dry or intermittent stream bed running through a
    canyon or gulley, usually a steep sided one. The term
    arroyo as used in the Southwestern United States has
    approximately the same meaning as the Arabic word
    wadi except that the latter is often used to denote very
    large water systems, i. e. , Wadi Hanifa, Wadi Fatima.

WADI SIRHAN PROJECT. One of the earlier agricultural
    experiments of the Saudi government, launched in 1957-
    1958 with the aim of providing wells and arable land
    on which to settle Bedouin. The project has since been
    extended to the entire northern province.

WAHHAB see MUHAMMAD IBN ABDUL WAHHAB

WAHHABISM. The reform sect of the Hanbali school of
    Sunni jurisprudence begun by Muhammad ibn Abdul
    Wahhab in the 1730's. Muhammad and his followers
    called themselves Muwahhidun or Unitarians and origi-
    nally the term Wahhabi was used in scorn. It is now

the most widespread (though technically incorrect) term
for this movement.
   The Wahhabi movement has for the most part been
restricted to the Arabian Peninsula, and more especially to the Nejd. However, in the early nineteenth century the Menang Kabau of central Sumatra became converted through pilgrims to Mecca who contacted the
Wahhabis there. The Menang Kabau then impressed
the creed onto the nearby Batak peoples leading to a
violent outbreak that was finally put down by Dutch
colonial armies.

WALLIN, GEORGE AUGUSTUS. Swedish explorer sent to
   the province of Jabal Shammar in 1845 by Muhammad
   Ali of Egypt, to make a reconaissance of Rashidi power. Wallin again explored parts of northern Arabia in
   1848.

WARAL. Arab name for the desert monitor found in Saudi
   Arabia. This carnivorous reptile is the largest of all
   the Arabian lizards.

WATER RESOURCES AND DEVELOPMENT. Since the for-
   mation of the Saudi state there has been a great deal
   of attention given to water projects and the Saudi Ministry of Agriculture, with a budget of some eighty-five
   million dollars, spends a considerable part of it on
   water control. In order to ascertain water resources,
   the Saudi government in the mid-1960's began a long
   term project of surveying and mapping the various parts
   of the kingdom. As of 1972, survey work had been
   completed on six of eight districts and was continuing
   on the remaining two. District one is the area of the
   Nafud and the Wadi Sirhan area, districts two and
   three are in eastern Asir and the large wadi systems
   draining eastward from the Asir highlands, districts
   four and five contain the Hasa and eastern Nejd and
   district six, the larger part of the Hejaz. District
   seven (Rub al Khali) and eight (western Nejd) have not
   been as yet completely surveyed. At present considerable attention is being given to the area of the central
   Wadi Hanifa, especially around Riyadh, which has by far
   the fastest growth rate in all of Arabia.
      Water projects include drilling of artesian and sur-
   face wells and the construction of dams. As of 1970
   major dams had been constructed in several areas including the vicinities of Riyadh, Taif, and Medina while

large dams were under construction near Abha in the
Asir highlands and in the Wadi Jizan in coastal Asir.
This latter project was developed by the German company Hoektiff and an Italian firm, Ital-Consult beginning in 1967. The Wadi Jizan dam has an estimated
capacity of a billion and a half cubic feet.
One very serious problem in post-war Saudi Arabia
is that of drinking water. The very rapid growth of
urban centers, especially of such cities as Riyadh and
Jedda has put a considerable strain on the ability of
the Saudi government to meet the needs of urban citi-
zens. Deep wells are used particularly at Riyadh but
considerable attention is now given to desalination of
sea water with plants at Jedda (considered the largest
in the world) which produces five million gallons of
water daily. An even larger plant is projected for
Khobar with a capacity of seven and a half million gallons per day, plus other smaller plants.
Two small pilot plants have already been constructed
at al Wajh and at Duba. Since 1965 a special Sea Water Desalination Department within the Ministry of Agriculture and Water has been formed and is directing
desalination activity.

-Y-

YAMAMA. An old town, dating from the early Islamic period, in the Wadi Hanifa southeast of Riyadh. Yamama,
at present, consists of scattered hamlets in the region
formed by the junction of the Wadi Nisa with the Wadi
Hanifa.

YANBU   see YENBO

YATHRIB   see MEDINA

YATIB, MOUNTAIN OF. An area near Hail where Saudi
archaeologists have discovered remains of ancient villages.

YEMEN. Independent nation in the southeastern part of the
peninsula. Yemen consists of an area of some 75,290
square miles and has a population of some four and a
half million people. The capital is at Sana in the highlands with a population of some 50,000. Other important cities include Taiz, south and west of Sana (popu-

lation ca. 12, 000) in the mountainous interior of Yemen. The chief peak in this Yemen range rises to 12, 336 feet, the highest point in the Arabian Peninsula. Yemen was under Turkish control till the end of World War I, at which time an independent state was set up under the Imam Yahya. In 1958 Yemen became federated with the United Arab Republic. The political situation in Yemen is at present very confused with a revolutionary government controlling the coastal areas and a member of Yahya's family holding parts of the interior. See also ARABIA, HISTORY OF--ISLAMIC PERIOD.

YENBO (Yenbu or Yanbu). Red Sea port that serves the Hejaz city of Medina.

-Z-

ZAHRA. Plant in the Rub al Khali area considered excellent food for camels. Tribulus sp.

ZAKAT. An obligatory tax (something like the Christian tithe) imposed on Moslems. Zakat means "purification" and indicates that the payment purifies the remaining property of the person involved. The tax varies, for example, on non-irrigated crops, it is 10%, on irrigated crops, 5%, and on money 2 1/2%. The tax is intended for charitable purposes and in the days of the early caliphate was collected by the government. Today it is normally a voluntary religious duty.

ZALUL. A racing camel. Such animals are extremely valuable and much care is spent on their selection and breeding.

ZAMIL IBN SUBHAN. Cousin of Hamud ibn Subhan and member of the influential Hail family that, in 1909, restored the ten year old Saud ibn Abdul Aziz to the throne. After the death of his cousin Hamud, Zamil became the regent for Saud.

ZAMZAM. The sacred well, revered both in pre-Islamic and in Islamic times, located near the Kaaba in Mecca. Zamzam is supposed to have supplied water to Ishmael, son of Abraham and his mother Hagar.

ZUHAIR.   Great pre-Islamic poet, who served an apprenticeship as a rawie.   See also RAWIE.

BIBLIOGRAPHY

-A-

Abercrombie, Thomas J. "Saudi Arabia: Beyond the Sands of Mecca." National Geographic, vol. 129, no. 1. (1966), p. 1-53.

Alexander, Jon. "Saudi Arabia: Significant aspects for Americans." M. A. thesis, Southern Illinois University Department of Government, 1962.

"The Arab World and Islam," Arab World, vol. 3, no. 2 (May-June 1957), p. 3-4.

Arnold, Sir Thomas W. The Caliphate. New York: Barnes & Noble, 1966.

Asimov, Isaac. The Near East; 10,000 Years of History. Boston: Houghton Mifflin, 1968.

Assah, Ahmed. Miracle of the Desert Kingdom. London: Johnson, 1969.

"Astraea of the Desert," Arab World, vol. 3, no. 3 (1957), p. 4-5.

-B-

Babun, Edward. "The Bedouin Arab: Unique Product of the Arabian Desert." Arab World, vol. 13, no. 4-5 (April-May 1967), p. 10-12.

Blau, Joshua. The Emergence and Linguistic Background of Judaeo-Arabic. New York: Oxford University Press, 1965.

Boase, Frederick. Modern English Biography. New York: Barnes & Noble, 1965.

123

Brown, William Robinson. The Horse of the Desert. New York: Macmillan, 1948.

Burckhardt, John Lewis. Notes on the Bedouins and Wahabys. London: H. Colburn and R. Bently, 1831.

Burton, Sir Richard Francis. Personal Narrative of a Pilgrimage to al-Madinah and Mecca, ed. by Isabel Burton. New York: Dover Pub., 1964.

Butler, Grant C. Kings and Camels. New York: Devin-Adair Co., 1961.

_____. Beyond Arabian Sands. New York: Devin-Adair Co., 1964.

Bouquet, A. C. Sacred Books of the World. Baltimore: Penguin, 1954.

-C-

Chejne, Anwar G. The Arabic Language; Its Role in History. Minneapolis: University of Minnesota Press, 1969.

Cole, J. P. Geography of World Affairs. Baltimore: Penguin Books, 1963 (A Pelican Original).

-D-

Dickson, Harold Richard Patrick. Writing. London: Thames and Hudson, 1951.

Diqs, Issak. A Bedouin Boyhood. New York: Praeger, 1969.

Djambatan Uitgeversbedrijf, N. V. Atlas of the Arab World and the Middle East. Amsterdam: Djambatan, 1960.

Doe, D. Brian. Socotra: An Archaeological Reconnaissance in 1967. Miami, Fla.: Field Research Projects, 1970.

_____. Southern Arabia. New York: McGraw-Hill, 1971.

Doughty, Charles. Travels in Arabia Deserta. New York: Heritage Press, 1953.

-E-

Encyclopaedia Britannica, 1910-11. New York: Cambridge
University Press.

_____, 1962. William Benton, Publisher.

_____, 1970. William Benton, Publisher.

Encyclopedia of Islam, 1959. Leiden: E. J. Brill

Esin, Emel. Mecca the Blessed Madinah the Radiant.
New York: Crown Pub., 1963.

Ettinghausen, Richard. A Selected and Annotated Bibliography of Books and Periodicals in Western Languages
Dealing with the Near and Middle East with Special
Emphasis on Medieval and Modern Times. Supplement. Washington, D. C.: Middle East Institute,
1954.

-F-

Fedden, Robin. English Travellers in the Near East. New
York: Longmans, Green, 1958.

Field, Henry. Bibliographies on Southwestern Asia.
Coral Gables, Fla.: University of Miami Press, n.d.

Finnie, David H. Pioneers East; the Early American Experience in the Middle East. Cambridge, Mass.:
Harvard University Press, 1967.

Firth, John Victor. The Middle East; a Geographical Note-
book. London: G. G. Harrap, 1963.

Fisher, William Bayne. The Middle East; A Physical,
Social, and Regional Geography. New York: Dutton,
1963.

Freeman-Grenville, G. S. P. The Muslim and Christian
Calendars. London: Oxford University Press, 1963.

-G-

Gaury, Gerald de. Rulers of Mecca. London: George G.
Harrap and Co., 1951.

125

_____. Faisal: King of Saudi Arabia. New York: Frederick A. Praeger, 1967.

Gibb, H. A. R. Mohammadism: An Historical Survey. New York: New American Library, 1955 (A Mentor Book).

_____. Studies on the Civilization of Islam. Boston: Beacon Press, 1962.

Glueck, Nelson. Rivers in the Desert: A History of Negev. New York: Farrar, Straus and Cudahy, 1959.

Great Britain. Naval Intelligence Division. Western Arabia and the Red Sea. London: Oxford University Press, 1946.

Guillaume, Alfred. Islam. Baltimore: Penguin Books, 1954.

-H-

Hansen, Thorkild. Arabia Felix, the Danish Expedition of 1761-1767, Trans. by James and Kathleen McFarlane. New York: Harper and Row, 1964.

Hazard, Harry W. Atlas of Islamic History, 2nd ed. Princeton, N. J.: Princeton University Press, 1952 (Princeton Oriental Studies, vol. 12).

Hitti, Philip Khuri. The Arabs, A Short History. New York: Gateway Edition, 1949.

_____. History of the Arabs. London: Macmillan and Co.; New York: St. Martin's Press, 1964.

Hogarth, David George. The Life of Charles M. Doughty. London: Oxford University Press, 1928.

_____. The Penetration of Arabia. Beirut: Khayats, 1966.

Howarth, David. The Desert King; A Life of Ibn Saud. London: Collins, 1964.

Hurgronje, Christiaan Snouck. Mekka in the Latter Part of the Nineteenth Century, trans. by J. H. Monaham (1931 ed.). Leiden: Brill, 1970.

Hyamson, Albert M. A Dictionary of Universal Biography. London: Routledge and Kegan Paul, 1951.

-I-

Ingrams, Harold. The Yemen. Imans, Rulers, and Revolutions. New York: Frederick A. Praeger, 1963.

International Travel Guide. African, Middle and Far East Holiday. New York: Continental Holiday, 1970.

-J-

Jacobsen, Hermann. A Handbook of Succulent Plants. London: Blandford Press, 1960.

Jarvis, C. S. Three Deserts. New York: E. P. Dutton, 1960.

Jeffrey, Arthur. Islam: Mohammad and His Religion. New York: Liberal Arts Press, 1958.

_____. A Reader on Islam. The Hague: Mouton and Co., 1962 (series A, no. 2).

-K-

Kelly, John Barrett. Eastern Arabian Frontiers. London: Faber and Faber, 1964.

Kheirallah, George. Arabia Reborn. Albuquerque: University of New Mexico Press, 1952.

Knightley, Phillip and Colin Simpson. The Secret Lives of Lawrence of Arabia. New York: McGraw-Hill (Bantam Books), 1971.

-L-

Landau, Rom. Arab Heritage of Western Civilization. Arab Information Center, Info. paper no. 20, 1962.

Landen, Robert Green. Oman Since 1856: Disruptive Modernization in a Traditional Arab Society. Princeton, N. J.: Princeton University Press, 1967.

Langer, William. An Encyclopedia of World History. Boston: Houghton Mifflin, 1940.

127

Lebkicher, Roy, George Rentz and Max Steineke. The
Arabia of Ibn Saud. New York: Russell F. Moore
Co., 1952.

_____. Aramco Handbook. New York: Arabian Ameri-
can Oil Co., 1960.

Levy, Reuben. The Social Structure of Islam. Cambridge,
England: University Press, 1965.

Lipsky, George Arthur. Saudi Arabia: Its People, Its
Society, Its Culture. New Haven, Conn.: HRAF
Press, 1959.

-M-

Mann, Major Clarence. Abu Dhabi: Birth of an Oil
Sheikhdom. Beirut: Khayats, 1964.

"The Meaning of Sufism," Arab World, vol. 3, no. 2 (May-
June 1957), p. 15-17.

Meinertzhagen, Richard. The Birds of Arabia. Edinburgh:
Oliver and Boyd, 1954.

Meulen, Daniel van der. The Wells of Ibn Sa'ud. New
York: Praeger, 1957.

Morgan, Kenneth W., ed. Islam: The Straight Path.
New York: Ronald Press Co., 1958.

-N-

"New Country, Old Problems," Newsweek, Dec. 13, 1971,
p. 50.

Nicholson, Margaret E. People in Books. New York:
H. W. Wilson Co., 1967.

Nicholson, Reynold A. A Literary History of the Arabs.
Cambridge, England: University Press, 1969.

North, C. R. An Outline of Islam. London: Epworth
Press, 1952.

Nutting, Anthony. The Arabs. New York: Clarkson N.
Potter, 1964.

- P -

Palgrave, William Gifford. <u>Narrative of a Year's Journey Through Central and Eastern Arabia.</u> London: Macmillan and Co., 1866.

Peterson, Emil Gustave. "Saudi Arabia in World Affairs." M. A. thesis, Southern Illinois University Department of Government, 1965.

Philby, H. St. John B. <u>Arabia.</u> New York: Scribner, 1930.

_____. <u>A Pilgrim in Arabia.</u> London: R. Hale, 1946.

_____. <u>Saudi Arabia.</u> New York: Praeger, 1955.

_____. <u>Forty Years in the Wilderness.</u> London: R. Hale, 1957.

Phillips, L. B. <u>Dictionary of Biographical Reference.</u> Graz, Austria: Akademische Druck, 1966.

Phillips, Wendell. <u>Oman: A History.</u> New York: Reynal and Company, in assoc. with William Morrow and Co., 1967.

Pickthall, Mohammad Marmaduke. <u>The Meaning of the Koran.</u> New York: New American Library, 1953 (A Mentor Book).

- R -

Rabon, Chaim. <u>Ancient West-Arabian.</u> London: Taylor's Foreign Press, 1951.

Rahman, Fazlur. <u>Islam.</u> New York: Holt, Rinehart, and Winston, 1966.

Raswan, Carl R. <u>Black Tents of Arabia.</u> New York: Creative Age Press, 1947.

Raunkiaer, Barclay. <u>Through Wahhibiland on Camelback.</u> New York: Praeger, 1969.

Rechinger, K. H. <u>Flora of Lowland Iraq.</u> New York: Hafner Pub. Co., 1964.

Riches, Phyllis M. An Analytical Bibliography of Universal Collected Biography. London: The Library Association, 1934.

Riley, Carroll L. The Origins of Civilization. Carbondale, Ill.: Southern Illinois University Press, 1969.

Rosenthal, E. I. J. Political Thought in Medieval Islam. Cambridge, England: University Press, 1958.

-S-

Sachar, Abram Leon. A History of the Jews. New York: Alfred A. Knopf, 1967.

Sale, George, Tr. and Ed. The Koran. New York: Hurst and Co., n. d.

Sanger, Richard Harlakenden. The Arabian Peninsula. Ithaca, N. Y.: Cornell University Press, 1954.

"Saudi Arabia," Arab World, vol. 4, no. 2-5 (1958), p. 33-36.

"Saudi Arabia," Arab World, vol. 9, no. 3 [Special Issue] (1965), p. 83-90.

Saudi Arabia. Ministry of Finance and National Economy. Statistical Yearbook. 1st ed., 1965; "6th issue," 1970.

Saudi Arabia. Ministry of Information. The Kingdom of Saudi Arabia: Facts and Figures. "Land Distribution and Settlement," 1971.

_____. _____. _____. "The Story of Education," 1971.

_____. _____. _____. "The Great Water Project," 1971.

_____. _____. _____. "The Plan of Social and Economic Development," 1971.

_____. _____. Saudi Arabia: Land of Achievement, n. d.

Saunders, J. J. A History of Medieval Islam. New York: Barnes and Noble, 1965.

Sharif, M. M. A History of Muslim Philosophy: I. Wiesbaden, Germany: O. Harrassowitz, 1963.

_____. A History of Muslim Philosophy: II. Wiesbaden: O. Harrassowitz, 1966.

Slocum, Robert S. Biographical Dictionaries and Related Works. Detroit: Gale Research Co., 1967.

Smith, Wilfred Cantwell. Islam in Modern History. Princeton, N. J.: Princeton University Press, 1957.

Smith, W. Robertson. Kinship and Marriage in Early Arabia. Boston: Beacon Press, 1903.

Somogy, Joseph de. "Arabia in World Trade," Arab World, vol. 5, no. 6 (July 1959), p. 12-13.

Sparrow, Judge Gerald. Modern Saudi Arabia. London: Knightley Vernon Ltd., 1970.

Stephen, Leslie and Sidney Lee. The Dictionary of National Biography. London: Oxford University Press, 1960.

Stewart, Desmond. Arab World. New York: Time, Inc., 1964. (Life-Time World Library).

"Styles from Saudi Arabia," Arab World, vol. 1, no. 11 (1956), p. 6-7.

-T-

Teghrarian, Souren. [Review of R. Bayly Winder's Saudi Arabia in the Nineteenth Century (New York, Macmillan)], Arab World, vol. 12, no. 9 (September 1966), p. 7.

Thesiger, Wilfred. Arabian Sands. New York: Dutton, 1959.

Thomas, Bertram. Arabia Felix: Across the "Empty Quarter" of Arabia. New York: Scribner, 1932.

_____. The Arabs. Garden City, N. Y.: Doubleday, Doran and Co., Inc., 1937.

Tweedie, Major General W. The Arabian Horse. Los Angeles: Borden Pub. Co., 1961.

Twitchell, Karl Saben. Saudi Arabia, with an Account of the Development of Its Natural Resources. Princeton, N. J.: Princeton University Press, 1958.

-V-

"Vacuum in the Gulf," Time, Feb. 7, 1972, p. 38-40.

Verhoeven, F. R. J. Islam; Its Origin and Spread in Words, Maps and Pictures. New York: St. Martin's Press, 1962.

Villiers, Alan. Sons of Sinbad. New York: Scribner, 1940.

-W-

Watt, W. Mongomery. Muhammad at Mecca. Oxford, England: Clarendon Press, 1953.

_____. Muhammad at Medina. Oxford, England: Clarendon Press, 1956.

Webster's Biographical Dictionary. Springfield, Mass.: G. & C. Merriam Co., 1966.

Wheeler, Sir Mortimer. Rome Beyond the Imperial Frontiers. Baltimore: Penguin Press, 1955 (A Pelican Book).

Who's Who in the Arab World. 1965/66.

Who's Who in the U. A. R. and the Near East. Cairo: 1954.

Who's Who in the World. Chicago: Marquis, 1971.

Wiese, Ernst. 10,000 Miles Through Arabia. London: Hale, 1968.

Williams, Kenneth. Ibn Sa'ud. London: Cape, 1933.

Williams, Neville. Chronology of the Modern World; 1763 to the Present Time. New York: David McKay Co., 1968.

Wilson, Sir Arnold. The Persian Gulf. London: Allen and Unwin, 1954.

Winder, R. Bayly. Saudi Arabia in the Nineteenth Century. London: Macmillan; New York: St. Martin's Press, 1965.

Wise, L. F. and E. W. Egan. Kings, Rulers and Statesmen. New York: Sterling Pub. Co., 1967.

World Muslim Congress. Some Economic Resources of Muslim Countries. Karachi: UMMA Pub. House, 1964.

-Y-

Yale, William. The Near East: A Modern History. Ann Arbor, Mich.: University of Michigan Press, 1968.